A QUEST FOR
MORE
SMALL GROUP AND
DISCUSSION GUIDE

A QUEST FOR
MORE
SMALL GROUP AND
DISCUSSION GUIDE

Living for something
bigger than you

PAUL DAVID TRIPP

New Growth Press
Greensboro, NC

Paul David Tripp, prolific author and international conference speaker, is president of Paul Tripp Ministries, whose mission is to educate and equip today's Christian by combining the in-depth study of God's Word with practical life applications. Tripp, also a pastor with over fifteen years of pastoral ministry, is adjunct professor at Westminster Theological Seminary and adjunct faculty member at the Christian Counseling and Educational Foundation in Glenside, Pennsylvania. He is the author of such best-selling titles as *Instruments in the Redeemer's Hands*, *War of Words*, *Age of Opportunity*, *Lost in the Middle*, and the co-author of *How People Change* and *Relationships: A Mess Worth Making*. Tripp has been married for thirty-five years and has four grown children.

New Growth Press, Greensboro, NC 27429
© 2008 by Paul David Tripp
All rights reserved. Published 2008

Cover Design: Ethan Tripp
Interior Design & Typesetting: Robin Black, www.blackbirdcreative.biz
Photo of Paul Tripp: David Sacks, www.davidsacks.com

Library of Congress Cataloging-in-Publication Data

Tripp, Paul David, 1950–
  A quest for more small group and discussion guide : living for something bigger than you /
Paul David Tripp.
    p. cm.
  Includes bibliographical references and index.
  ISBN 978-0-9785567-8-5
1. Church group work. 2. Small groups—Religious aspects—Christianity. I. Title.
  BV652.2.T75 2008
  268'.434—dc22

                              2008006231
Printed in Canada
08 09 10 11 12   5 4 3 2 1

CONTENTS

How to Use This Study Guide 7

1: A Quest for More 17

2: More or Less 25

3: A Total Disaster 33

   Where Have I Been: Chapters 1-3 40

4: Welcome to My Little Kingdom 43

5: Discovering Your Civilization 51

6: The Costume Kingdom 59

   Where Have I Been: Chapters 4-6 65

7: The Shrink Dynamic 67

8: In the Center of It All 73

9: Welcome to Your Death 81

   Where Have I Been: Chapters 7-9 86

10: The Jesus Focus 89

11: Groaning 93

12: Jazz 99

   Where Have I Been: Chapters 10-12 103

13: Forgiveness 105

14: Loneliness 109

15: Sacrifice 113

   Where Have I Been: Chapters 13-15 116

16: Anger 119

17: Hope 123

18: Putting It All Together 127

Bible Studies

One: Life in the Garden 131

Two: The Crown of Glory 134

Three: The Kingdom of Light. 136

Four: A Precious Death 139

Five: The Nature of a Kingdom Servant. 142

Six: The King's Treasure. 145

Seven: Jacob's Rescue. 147

A Quick Word About the Following Notes 150

Notes on Chapters 1-3 151

Notes on Chapters 4-6. 153

Notes on Chapters 7-9 155

Notes on Chapters 10-12 156

Notes on Chapters 13-15 157

Notes on Chapters 16-18 157

Notes on Bible Study One 158

Notes on Bible Study Two 160

Notes on Bible Study Three 161

Notes on Bible Study Four 163

Notes on Bible Study Five 164

Notes on Bible Study Six 165

Notes on Bible Study Seven 166

HOW TO USE THIS STUDY GUIDE ■■■■■■■■■■■■■■■■■■

By cultural definition he was a successful man. In a real way he had it all. He had been a star athlete. What he had accomplished in his business career was amazing. He lived in the mansion and drove the luxury cars that are image markers for successful people. He had provided the best of material things for his family. Yet, with all of the external success, this man was in my office because something was terribly wrong. His wife had recently moved out, and he had no relationship with his children whatsoever. Defeated and depressed over the explosion of his family, he began to fail at work as well and had just lost his job. I couldn't help but think of Harry as I wrote this book.

Harry's story defines how inaccurately our culture defines success. Harry discovered what many people feel, deep down inside, regardless of what advertisers and the culture tries to tell us—that there must be more to life than what can be gained in this world. In the process of counseling, Harry learned that the "more" he had been living for was actually less. He began learning how to live for something bigger than himself.

I am reminded that what we often call "success" and "the good life" still leaves us empty, depressed, unfocused, disillusioned, and disappointed. We were not hardwired to live for the best this world has to offer. God designed us for much more. God intends our lives to have meaning and purpose— to live in pursuit of more than just survival, more than just temporary pleasure, more even than just lives that are good. God intends for us to live lives that are eternally *great!* Lives that extend far beyond our small, personal worlds and connect to the very eternal and glorious purposes of God. This is the message of hope presented in *A Quest for More.*

This **Study Guide** will lead you through *A Quest for More,* highlighting key points by asking you to organize the content into your thinking and by asking you to evaluate your own life in relation to the truths presented.

It will also take you into Scripture to examine more deeply the principles and examples God has given us in his Word which can guide you to live the life God intends. Change in your life will not happen as effectively by just reading as it will if you interact with, question, and seek to apply what you are reading. This study is intended to help you interact, question, and apply the principles in *A Quest for More*.

The **Bible Study** sections are not just biblical support for *A Quest for More,* but rather they are intended to be a mirror, revealing our hearts and lives. Allow the Bible studies, in accordance with *A Quest for More,* to show you what God may want to change or improve in your life. It has been my experience that God often works in my heart one issue at a time. What about you? What is God preparing for you? What areas of your thinking does God want to correct or reinforce? What behaviors is God weeding out and what behaviors is God cultivating in you? The Holy Spirit, one of God's greatest gifts to you, is willing and able to reveal truth to you if you are willing to listen and examine your heart. Determine not to be just a listener of the Word but also a doer (James 1:22–24). God bless you as you seek him and his kingdom.

My special thanks to Michael Breece who worked so diligently with me to make this study guide what it is.

PAUL DAVID TRIPP

1. Read the chapters in *A Quest for More* that coincide with the chapters of this study.

2. The ***You Are Here*** questions are designed to have you think about key issues and to assess your life and thinking before you read. Thinking through these questions begins your interaction with the content and provides thoughts that will connect what you may already know or be doing with what is being presented in the book.

3. The questions for ***Looking at My Destination*** are designed to help you think through the content of each chapter and to reinforce key principles. You may want to have the Study Guide open in front of you as you read from *A Quest for More* and use the questions to focus your reading. Or you may want to read the entire chapter first and then go back and use the questions to reinforce and help you understand and organize the information in each chapter.

4. The questions for ***Deciding My Course*** are intended for you to apply the general ideas and principles of each chapter to the specific circumstances of your life. Take time to pray as you answer these questions and evaluate yourself. Be honest and transparent with yourself and with God. Keep reminding yourself that God's grace is sufficient for you.

5. Some of the chapters include ***Points of Interest*** that will take you deeper into the content and principles or will provide you an opportunity to reinforce and apply key principles in a different

way than just thinking about them. Although the principles from *A Quest for More* can be understood and applied apart from these questions and activities, the questions and activities in this section are extremely valuable and can reap tremendous insights.

6. The **Bible Studies** will connect various biblical passages to similar themes in the book. They are intended to be done in conjunction with the book as you read, but they could be done before or after you read the book. Where each *Bible Study* could fit within the scope of the whole study is found within the *Points of Interest* as well as the *Bible Studies* themselves.

7. At the end of every three chapters, there is a **Where Have I Been** section designed for you to review and reinforce key principles. Taking the time to do this section will help the key principles remain in your memory and remind you of what you can be applying to your life.

USING THIS STUDY GUIDE: FOR SMALL GROUP STUDY ■ ■ ■

1. Although the lessons and chapters can be used and adjusted to meet the needs or purposes of the group, the chapters in *A Quest for More* and the sections in the Study Guide are intended to be read and answered individually, then discussed within a small group setting. The **Bible Studies** are intended to be done within the small group together. There is also a suggested order explained below, but this too can be adjusted to the needs and purposes of the group.

2. The ***Where Have I Been*** section is designed as the primary means of review and discussion for the small group. The questions should cover the key principles, but there is also a place for the group to consider any of the questions in the study sections.

3. The ***Bible Studies*** are designed to connect God's Word to important themes of the book. The studies are intended and designed to be done in the small group setting together, but can also be done individually, if desired.

4. The ***Setting Up Camp*** section is designed to apply key principles to the group as a whole.

5. There is a place for the small group to check up on itself and to ensure that each member is keeping up, understanding, and benefiting from the reading. This is an important aspect of small groups and, if possible, should not be ignored.

RECOMMENDED STUDY GUIDE OUTLINE ■ ■ ■ ■ ■ ■ ■ ■ ■ ■ ■ ■

I recommend you follow the 13-Lesson Outline; however, the study can certainly be beneficial no matter how you decide to work through it. Consider your or your small group's needs and purposes and then decide on a plan.

Using the Study Guide in a small group or Sunday school setting is recommended because it allows you to think more deeply about the principles as you discuss them with others. Also, a small group provides encouragement and accountability. If you are not reading *A Quest for More* along with a small group, perhaps you can find at least one other person who will also read the book and complete the guide with you.

The 13-Lesson Outline is recommended because it can cover the eighteen chapters of the book in thirteen weeks. Also the 13-Lesson Outline weaves together the individual study, the group discussion, and the Bible studies so that there is a connection between all three sections. It fosters a level of variety so that there is time to think about what you are reading and a time to take a break from just reading and discussing.

13-LESSON OUTLINE ■

This outline is presented for a small group format. If you are doing the study individually, all the lesson components can be completed at home in the same order. For small groups, the outline has a component to be completed at home by the individual and a component to be completed in the small group together. The first lesson will begin together in the small group.

Lesson One

At group— Bible Study One: *Life in the Garden*

At home— Read chapters 1 and 2 in *A Quest for More*. Answer the questions in the Study Guide for chapters 1 and 2.

Lesson Two

At group— Group Check-Up/Bible Study Two: *The Crown of Glory*

At home— Read chapter 3 in *A Quest for More*. Answer the questions in the Study Guide for chapter 3. Be prepared to share your answers and ideas when your small group meets.

Lesson Three

At group— Complete *Where Have I Been* for chapters 1–3.

At home— Read chapters 4 and 5 in *A Quest for More*. Answer the questions in the Study Guide for chapters 4 and 5.

Lesson Four

At group— Group Check-Up/Bible Study Three: *The Kingdom of Light*

At home— Read chapter 6 in *A Quest for More*. Answer the questions in the Study Guide for chapter 6. Be prepared to share your answers and ideas when your small group meets.

Lesson Five

At group— Complete *Where Have I Been* for chapters 4–6.

At home— Read chapters 7 and 8 in *A Quest for More*. Answer the questions in the Study Guide for chapters 7 and 8.

Lesson Six

At group— Group Check-Up/Bible Study Four: *A Precious Death*

At home— Read chapter 9 in *A Quest for More*. Answer the questions in the Study Guide for chapter 9. Be prepared to share your answers and ideas when your small group meets.

Lesson Seven

At group— Complete *Where Have I Been* for chapters 7–9.

At home— Read chapters 10 and 11 in *A Quest for More*. Answer the questions in the Study Guide for chapters 10 and 11.

Lesson Eight

At group— Group Check-Up/Bible Study Five: *The Nature of a Kingdom Servant*

At home— Read chapter 12 in *A Quest for More*. Answer the
questions in the Study Guide for chapter 12. Be
prepared to share your answers and ideas when your
small group meets.

Lesson Nine

At group— Complete *Where Have I Been* for chapters 10–12.

At home— Read chapters 13 and 14 in *A Quest for More*.
Answer the questions in the Study Guide for
chapters 13 and 14.

Lesson Ten

At group— Group Check-Up/Bible Study Six: *The King's
Treasure*

At home— Read chapter 15 in *A Quest for More*. Answer the
questions in the Study Guide for chapter 15.
Be prepared to share your answers and ideas when
your small group meets.

Lesson Eleven

At group— Complete *Where Have I Been* for chapters 13–15.

At home— Read chapters 16 and 17 in *A Quest for More*.
Answer the questions in the Study Guide for
chapters 16 and 17.

Lesson Twelve

At group— Group Check-Up/Bible Study Seven: *The Great Rescue*

At home— Read chapter 18 in *A Quest for More*. Answer the
questions in the Study Guide for chapter 18. Be
prepared to share your answers and ideas when your
small group meets.

Lesson Thirteen

At group— Complete *Where Have I Been* for chapters 16–18.

SUGGESTIONS FOR A SUCCESSFUL SMALL GROUP MEETING ■

1. Agree on a beginning and ending time, and then begin and end on time.
2. Be prepared. Know which questions you want to ask and have your thoughts prepared.
3. Be flexible. The study is not necessarily the most important thing; if someone in the group has a different need or concern, set the study aside.
4. Keep the group focused. A successful group needs a leader. Bring the group back to the study if it strays into other topics.
5. Allow "wait time." Give the group time to think about a question you ask. Avoid answering the question yourself. If it seems necessary, ask the question again in a different way.
6. Solicit multiple answers. Even if someone answers a question, ask someone else what he/she thinks. For some questions it is even appropriate to go around to every person and get his/her answer. This can generate good discussion. However, don't force anyone to answer.
7. Be affirming of everyone's answers. If an answer seems incorrect or "unbiblical" ask the person to support his/her idea or ask the rest of the group, "What do you all think?" It is acceptable to leave a question unanswered or unresolved. Move forward and later discussion may resolve or answer the question. If you reject someone's answer or allow someone in the group to reject someone's answer, most people will then be less likely to share their ideas.

8. Be sincere and open. The group will most likely follow your lead.

WHAT IS A GROUP CHECK-UP? ■

Every other week, it can be very beneficial to obtain feedback from the members of the group.

- Have them write down on a note card any questions they have at this point or struggles they are having with reading/ understanding. Using the cards saves time while allowing everyone the chance to communicate.

- On a separate note card have members write down things they have been challenged by, changed in, or working toward as a result of their reading.

- Set aside the second set of note cards. Look quickly at the first set of cards and identify any needs that should be addressed right away.

- If there are no immediate needs, let the group know that you will look more closely at the questions and then discuss them the next time you meet when you will also share the comments on the second set of cards.

1: A QUEST FOR MORE

1. God's purpose for our lives is to transcend our self-oriented existence and to be part of something bigger than just our own survival and our own little definition of happiness. In each of us, God has created a desire to live for more than ourselves and to be a part of God's kingdom of glory. When our lives are connected to God's transcendent glories, our lives have purpose and will make a difference.

2. There are four transcendent glories our lives were created to focus on: God's glory, stewardship glory, community glory, and truth glory.
   a. All things—including stewardship, community, and truth glories—and all people were created to be connected to **God glory.** There is no higher or greater glory than God himself.
   b. **Stewardship glory** is the glory to which we are called to transcend our miniscule, individual kingdoms by ruling and caring for God's immense creation.

    c. **Community glory** is the transcendent glory we share when we live in community with one another.

    d. **Truth glory** is the invitation to transcend the boundaries of our own thoughts, interpretations, and experiences and to share in God's revealed knowledge.

3. The immediate, mundane details of life can tempt us to settle for less than God's glory by leading our focus away from God's kingdom and God's transcendent glories toward our own kingdoms. Living for God's glories does not mean abandoning the immediate, mundane details of life, but rather living for God's glories where he has placed us in the immediate, mundane details of life. It is in this way that our lives will have purpose.

CHAPTER GOALS ■■■■■■■■■■■■■■■■■■■■■■■■■■■■■

1. The beginning goal of chapter 1 is to begin to see that our lives were created to be part of something much bigger than just ourselves—more than just our own survival and our own pleasures.

2. The other goal, therefore, of this chapter is for us to consider how our normal, everyday lives should connect with the transcendent glories of God, stewardship, community, and truth.

3. We want to look at our big vision for our lives and evaluate that vision against God's vision for our lives.

■ ■ ■ ■ ■

You Are Here

1. Do you tend to see your life more as meaningful or meaningless?
2. When do you experience times of meaningfulness?
3. Do you believe you were created to be part of something big?
4. What might be the greatest thing you have accomplished in life so far?
5. What made it so great?
6. In what ways do you believe you make a difference?
7. If you had it all, what would "all" look like?

Looking at My Destination

1. Why is a desire for world peace or solving world hunger uniquely human?

2. What does it mean to transcend the boundaries of our average world?

3. Give two reasons why we, as humans, desire transcendence.

4. For what kind of transcendence did God *not* make us? For what kind were we made?

5. What does the author mean by "narrowing the size of our lives to the size of our own existence"? If we narrow the size of our lives to the size of our own existence, why is it a denial of our humanity?

> ■ ■ ■ ■ ■
>
> WE WERE NEVER
> MEANT TO BE
> SELF-FOCUSED
> LITTLE KINGS RULING
> MINISCULE LITTLE
> KINGDOMS
> WITH A POPULATION
> OF ONE.
>
> ■ ■ ■ ■ ■

6. How is it possible to live a "Christian life" while settling for "below and less" instead of living for "above and more"?

7. What does God invite us to that is more than a better marriage, a better relationship with our children, or better success at work?

8. What does it mean to be a "glory junkie"? Is this good or bad?

9. Is it enough to have purpose? What should be the connection between purpose and glory?

10. What are the four transcendent glories for which we were created?

11. How can we pursue the glory of God?

12. How do the four transcendent glories call us out of the "tight confines of a self-oriented existence" to something "above and beyond"?

13. Since we are called and created by God to live beyond the normal and routine, why shouldn't we stop doing all the normal and routine activities of our days?

DECIDING MY COURSE ■

1. How do you see a desire for transcendence in the lives of other people? In yourself? What is something you do or have done because it provides an opportunity to transcend the "small boundaries" of your average world?

2. If you had no financial or physical obstacles, what great feat would you want to accomplish?

3. What is your "boldest and most expansive dream"? Does it fit the vision of transcendence or does it only fit your own "miniscule little kingdom"?

4. What is the difference between someone who lives a purposeful life apart from God and one who lives a purposeful life connected to seeking God's transcendent glories? Which most characterizes you?

5. Which of the four transcendent glories do you participate in the most? The least?

6. What could you do to participate more in each of the transcendent glories?

7. What tends to make you lose sight of the "expansive, glorious, and eternal that is meant to give direction to everything you do"?

8. What big thing are you living for right now?

9. Think of an area or relationship in your life which you could expand to the size of God's transcendent glories. Think of specific ways you could connect this area or relationship to God's glory.

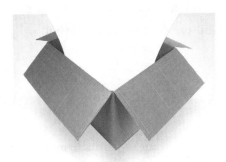

2: MORE OR LESS

1. We are all capable of fighting for what has little value, committed to our little kingdoms, while forgetting things of transcendent value.
2. When we opt for a "me-centered more," what we actually get is always much, much less because
    a. our humanity is connected to the glory of God and
    b. to disobey God or to shape our lives around normal, self-oriented concerns—instead of God's transcendent glories—will never lead to greater glory.
3. Knowing we were created to be connected to something more glorious than just our survival, Satan presents us with less in a way that makes it appear to be more.
4. Satan wins a victory every time he successfully tempts us to exchange the God-centered more for one of the "me-centered mores" that dangle before us in this fallen world.

5. Jesus came to rescue us from ourselves and free us to participate in his transcendence. Learning to live for the transcendent glories of God is a process, not an event.

CHAPTER GOALS ■■■■■■■■■■■■■■■■■■■■■■■■■■■■■■

1. In this chapter we want to be made aware that we all struggle in our daily, normal lives with settling for less, and we want to consider how we allow this to happen.
   a. We lose sight of God's transcendent glories and focus on "near" glories.
   b. We are tempted and deceived by the appearance of "more" which is actually less.
2. We want to understand why pursuing glory that is disconnected from God leads to less and not more and then apply that understanding to our lives by identifying the lesser things for which we settle.

■ ■ ■ ■ ■
You Are Here
List some legitimate concerns you face in your everyday life.

Looking at My Destination
1. Think back to chapter 1. What are the four things of transcendent value?

2. What are some of the examples of the minor details of life the author provides?

3. What is the war in which we are all involved?

4. Satan offered Eve an opportunity at transcendence. What was wrong in this?

5. How does Satan present us all with less in ways that appear to be more?

6. Explain why pursuing glory that is disconnected from God's glory leads to less, not more.

7. Using the examples from the section titled *It's Always the Same Old Set of Tricks,* explain how we can settle for less, thinking we are gaining more.

8. What is the basic lie Satan is telling us? Why is it only a lie?

> ■ ■ ■ ■ ■
>
> SATAN KNOWS THAT
> WE ALL HUNGER FOR
> TRANSCENDENCE,
> SO HIS CRAFT IS TO
> PRESENT US WITH
> LESS IN A WAY THAT
> APPEARS TO BE MORE.
>
> ■ ■ ■ ■ ■

9. Why are the little moments of life so significant?

10. What is a "shadow glory"? How are these "shadow glories" like spiritual crack?

11. Explain the struggle in which we consistently find ourselves.

12. How can a legitimate concern become a spiritual danger?

13. According to the author, why has God sent his Redeemer Son to earth?

14. In what ways are we restored to God glory? To community glory? To stewardship glory? To truth glory?

DECIDING MY COURSE ■■■■■■■■■■■■■■■■■■■■■■■■■

1. Think of a time in the past, or something currently, when you treated a minor detail of life as if it were a major thing? What was the pseudo-glory you were tempted by? What could you have done differently so that your response was tied to God's transcendent glories?

2. What are some "near glories" that claimed your focus this past week?

> ■ ■ ■ ■ ■
>
> LEARNING TO
> LIVE WITH THE
> TRANSCENDENT
> GLORIES OF GOD IS
> A PROCESS,
> NOT AN EVENT.
>
> ■ ■ ■ ■ ■

3. Can you think of a time when you achieved "less," thinking you were gaining "more"?

4. Examine the past few weeks. What is the "more" for which you were questing?

5. What behavior-shaping or decision-making events in your life do you need to connect to God's transcendent glories? How can you do this?

6. Look back at your list of concerns (You Are Here). In how many mundane ways each week are you tempted to compress the size of your living to the concerns of your life? How can you focus yourself to expand those concerns to the size of God's glory?

7. Identify evidence of the struggle in your life to go after less as if it were more—in your times of leisure, at work, with your family, at church, or in your small group.

8. Is there a place for independence in the Christian life?

9. How does it make you feel knowing that God created you to participate in his glory?

■■■■■

What a thought! God has created us to participate in his glory! Certainly we want to obey God and live up to his expectation, but as you consider the areas of your life that do not live up to his expectation, you may begin to feel incapable or incompetent. Don't give up! First John 5:3–4 says,

This is love for God: to obey his commands. *And his commands are not burdensome,* for everyone born of God *overcomes the world.* This is the victory that has overcome the world, even our faith (emphasis added).

POINTS OF INTEREST ■■■■■■■■■■■■■■■■■■■■■■■■■■■

1. Complete **Bible Study Two:** *The Crown of Glory.*
2. Read Matthew 4:1–11. How is what Satan offers Jesus "less"? Where is Jesus' focus in being able to resist Satan's temptation? How can we apply this event to our lives in helping us to resist Satan's lies?
3. Read Numbers 11:4–35. How have the people reduced the glory of God to the size of their own lives? What does God do to remind them of the size of his glory?
4. Read Exodus 32:1–35. How do the actions of the people cause them to lose out on God's glory (32:1–4)? Stewardship glory (vv. 3–4, 20)? Community glory (vv. 25, 28)? Truth glory (vv. 15–19)?

5. Read Luke 22:24–30 and John 13:12–17. What is Jesus teaching us about living for his kingdom?

6. Read Galatians 2:11–14. Are you able to relate at all with Peter? Have you ever let fear or your reputation take prominence over God's transcendent glories?

3: A TOTAL DISASTER

1. Adam and Eve's disobedience forever tarnished God's creation, but the greatest catastrophe was the loss of transcendence, meaning, and purpose.
2. Just like Adam and Eve, our quest for autonomy will always crush transcendence.
3. Autonomy is a replacement glory that does not result in transcendence but in guilt, fear, and death. Sin pulls us away from God and toward ourselves and shrinks the boundaries of glory. God's grace rescues us from our confined lives to participate in the vast expanse of the kingdom of God; however, God's work of grace is not yet done in our lives.
4. God's agenda is not just for our own personal benefit or to make our own little kingdoms successful, but rather we are redeemed for the purpose of being a part of the glory of God and of his work of making *everything* new.

CHAPTER GOALS ■■■■■■■■■■■■■■■■■■■■■■■■■■■■■■

1. In this chapter, we want to accurately view the desire for autonomy as a lie and a great tragedy that actually shrinks the boundaries of glory and results in guilt, fear, and death.
2. We want to evaluate whether we, even as Christians, live in God's grace only to make our own little kingdoms successful, instead of living for the greater glory of God.
3. We want to evaluate whether we are mainly living for our own redemption instead of living for God's work of redemption in everything.

■■■■■

You Are Here
1. What are your favorite aspects of God's creation?
2. If you could pick one or two causes of suffering to eliminate, what would they be?
3. What is often seen as the good life? Is the "good life" different for Christians than it is for non-Christians?
4. Who would you say benefits the most from your salvation—you or others?

Looking at My Destination
1. Why was the fall of Adam and Eve not just an error, but a catastrophe?

2. Explain the tragedy we find in Genesis 3:8–10.

3. What is a "replacement glory"?

4. What was the lie Satan told Adam and Eve?

5. Why is autonomy not true transcendence?

6. What does the author mean by the inertia of sin?

7. What has God done and continued to do to help us in our battle against autonomy?

8. What are some examples the author provides of our battle with autonomy and living for God's transcendence? Can you think of other examples?

9. Why is it important to remember that God's work of grace is not done yet?

10. What is the purpose of God's grace in our lives?

11. What does it mean to "Christianize" our autonomy?

12. What does it mean to live with the total restoration of creation in view? Why and how are we as Christians to live in light of this purpose?

13. How do we sometimes alter and lessen the greater goal of redemption?

14. What can cause us to do that?

DECIDING MY COURSE ■■■■■■■■■■■■■■■■■■■■■■■■■■

1. In what way is an act of disobedience I may commit as much a catastrophe as Adam and Eve's disobedience?

2. Review the author's descriptions of the effects of the fall. Which of the effects do you identify with the most right now in your life's situations?

3. Have you ever, in some way, "hidden" (or are you now hiding) yourself or some part of yourself from God? What was (or is) the glory you were chasing after that resulted in your "hiding"?

4. Why do you think God's work of grace is a process and not just an automatic event?

> ■■■■■
>
> YOUR CELEBRATION OF GOD'S RESTORING GRACE SHOULD BE BIGGER THAN THE FACT THAT IT BRINGS BLESSING TO YOUR PRIVATE WORLD.
>
> ■■■■■

5. Take time to think about the past week. Identify times when you were living for yourself. Confess these times to the Lord and remind yourself that God's grace is sufficient and the process is not done yet.

6. Examine and ask God to reveal to you whether you are still focused on your own autonomy (a "Christianized" autonomy). How can you begin to become more a part of God's purpose in making *everything* new (not just yourself)?

7. Identify some areas of your life where having it good has perhaps prevented you from seeking God's greater purposes.

8. At the beginning of the book you were asked what it would look like to "have it all." Do you think the borders of your "all" are too small?

9. Who do you think should benefit most from your salvation—you or others?

10. In view of the ideas from chapter 3, how would you define the opposite of autonomy?

11. Have you treated the size of God's grace as if it were no bigger than the size of your personal concerns?

POINT OF INTEREST ■

Read Hebrews 11. How do we see these "ancients" living for God's bigger kingdom and God's purpose of restoration? How do we see that we are a part of this grand purpose? (Consider vv. 39–40.)

WHERE HAVE I BEEN ■■■■■■■■■■■■■■■■■■■■■■■■■■■■■

Chapters 1–3

1. What does the author mean by "narrowing the size of our lives to the size of our own existence"?
2. What are the four transcendent glories for which we were created?
3. How do the four transcendent glories call us out of the "tight confines of a self-oriented existence" to something "above and beyond"?
4. Since we are called and created by God to live beyond the normal and routine, why shouldn't we stop doing all the normal and routine activities of our days?
5. What is the difference between someone who lives a purposeful life apart from God and one who lives a purposeful life connected to seeking God's transcendent glories?
6. What tends to make you lose sight of the "expansive, glorious, and eternal that is meant to give direction to everything you do"?
7. Explain the struggle in which we consistently find ourselves.
8. How can a legitimate concern become a spiritual danger?
9. In how many mundane ways each week are you tempted to compress the size of your living to the concerns of your life? How can we focus ourselves to expand those concerns to the size of God's glory?
10. What is a "replacement glory"?
11. What is the purpose of God's grace in our lives?
12. What does it mean to "Christianize" our autonomy?
13. What does it mean to live with the total restoration of creation in view?
14. In what way is an act of disobedience that I may commit as much a catastrophe as Adam and Eve's disobedience?
15. Why do you think God's work of grace is a process and not just an automatic event?

16. How is living for yourself an act of bondage and an act that shrinks the size of your life?

17. Leader: Read the questions and comments from the cards collected after chapter 2.

SETTING UP CAMP ■■■■■■■■■■■■■■■■■■■■■■■■■■■■■■

1. Is there a transcendent glory which the group could participate in more as a group? Come up with some ideas and apply them together as a group.

2. What is the vision for your group? Does it fit a vision of transcendence or is it limited to the needs and desires of the group? What could you do individually and as a group to stretch your vision to the size of God's vision?

3. Share a situation with your group that happened to you this past week and allow the group to provide answers on how you could have let God glory, stewardship glory, community glory, or truth glory give direction to your handling of the situation.

4. As a group, memorize 2 Corinthians 5:15.
   "And he died for all, that those who live should no longer live for themselves but for him who died for them and was raised again."

5. God has created us for transcendence, but it can feel discouraging if we truly see how far we fall from his expectation. Read together Ephesians 3:14–21 and 1 John 5:3–4. Discuss the encouragement we can find in these passages.

6. Allow time for people to share what they are learning. Ask if they have done any of the **Points of Interest** and if they would share what has come from that.

4: WELCOME TO
MY LITTLE KINGDOM

CORE PRINCIPLES ■■■■■■■■■■■■■■■■■■■■■■■■■■■■■

1. We are all kingdom builders. Everything we do is done in pursuit of the success of either God's kingdom or my own little kingdom. This pursuit is a commitment of the heart.

2. Little kingdom living is characterized by the pursuit of earth-bound treasures and anxiety-bound needs. Focusing on our needs leads to the needs-expansion dynamic: The more we live with the meeting of our needs as our central focus of concern, the more things in our lives get defined as needs.

3. Little kingdom living is characterized by placing ourselves and our desires as the focus of our decisions and actions. We are even capable of thinking we are living for God's kingdom while really still serving our own little kingdoms. Jesus taught us to seek first his kingdom and his righteousness (Matthew 6:33).

CHAPTER GOALS ■■■■■■■■■■■■■■■■■■■■■■■■■■■■■■

1. In chapter 4, we want to be made aware of what characterizes little kingdom living and evaluate ourselves in view of these characteristics.
2. We want to recognize where, even in our service to God, we are living more for our own kingdoms than we are for his.
3. We want to recognize things we define as needs, which probably are not, and begin to seek first God's kingdom in everything we do.

■■■■■

You Are Here

1. What are some things you have built in your life?
2. If you found a treasure at a yard sale, what would it be?
3. What makes a "good day" a good day for you?
4. What defines something to be a need? Reread Luke 4 from the perspective of needs. What things did Christ focus his needs on?
5. In your own words, define "kingdom."

Looking at My Destination

1. In what way are we all kingdom builders?

2. What is the war each of us is involved in every day?

3. Where and how can we participate in God's kingdom?

4. According to the author, what causes us to live more for our own kingdoms than God's kingdom?

5. According to Jesus' teaching in Matthew 6, why shouldn't we store up treasures on earth?

6. According to Jesus' teaching in Matthew 6, why shouldn't we worry about our life?

7. What two points of focus characterize "little kingdom living"?

8. In what way are we all treasure hunters? Why shouldn't we invest our time and resources in this world's "treasures"?

■ ■ ■ ■ ■

WITHOUT KNOWING IT, WE CAN REDUCE THE PROMISES OF SCRIPTURE DOWN TO A HOPE THAT GOD'S GRACE WILL ENSURE THE SUCCESS OF OUR LITTLE KINGDOMS.

■ ■ ■ ■ ■

9. Explain why or how the physical values of earth somehow become our treasures. (Think back to chapter 3.)

10. How does living for your own kingdom lead to anxiety?

11. How does living for your own kingdom dehumanize our lives?

12. What is the "need-expansion" dynamic?

13. Both God's kingdom and my personal little kingdom are commitments of the heart. How does this commitment shape the way I respond to everything?

14. How does little kingdom living crush our humanity?

15. For what purpose did God send a Redeemer? How can we even take advantage of this for our own kingdom?

16. How was it God's grace when God removed the author from such a cherished and influential position?

17. The author defines an old way and a new way of living. What are the differences between the two?

DECIDING MY COURSE ■

1. Whose kingdom did you fight for today?

2. Whose kingdom's successes do you most hope for—God's or your own?

3. In Matthew 6, Jesus refers to his listeners as "you of little faith." How does faith play a role in building God's kingdom?

4. What troubles in your life tend to cause you to worry? How can you seek first God's kingdom in these areas?

5. What are some treasures that you seek? If someone watched the video of your last year, what treasure would she/he conclude you are after? Material possessions, money, good health, secure future, success, acceptance, power, control, comfort?

   What can you do so these things are not your treasures?

6. Is there a place in your life where you are squeezing the big kingdom vision into your own little kingdom? What can you do to refocus your vision?

POINTS OF INTEREST ■■■■■■■■■■■■■■■■■■■■■■■■■■■

1. What treasures does Paul say he seeks in Philippians 3:7–14?

2. Can you find other passages of Scripture that define what our treasures should be?

5: DISCOVERING YOUR CIVILIZATION

CORE PRINCIPLES ■■■■■■■■■■■■■■■■■■■■■■■■■■■■■■■

1. We are always working to build some kind of civilization and culture, and we are always pressing the rules and values of that civilization onto others.
   a. Consequently, we have a tendency to not only build our own kingdoms but to also expect the people around us to live by the rules and to serve the purposes of our kingdoms.
   b. Our personal kingdom building can go unnoticed because it happens in the small, little-noticed moments of life and because we have defined biblical morality as the keeping of a set of rules.
2. We can mix big kingdom living and small kingdom rules.
3. Little kingdom living is characterized by self-focus, self-righteousness, self-satisfaction, self-reliance, self-rule, and self-glorification.

CHAPTER GOALS ■■■■■■■■■■■■■■■■■■■■■■■■■■■■■■■■■

1. In this chapter, we want to recognize what little kingdom living looks like so that it does not go unnoticed and so that we can live properly and wholly for God's kingdom.
2. We want to be freed from the sin that pulls us to focus on ourselves
   a. by remembering that it is for this freedom that Christ died and set us free;
   b. by remembering that we do not need to hide and justify our sin because, by Christ's death, our every sin is forgiven;
   c. by remembering that we have been given the Holy Spirit who enables us to say "no" to little kingdom desires; and
   d. by remembering that some day our kingdom conflicts will be over.

■■■■■

You Are Here
1. What do you think of when you think of being civilized?
2. If an archaeologist "dug into your world," what discoveries and conclusions would be made?

Looking at My Destination
1. In what way are we all "civilizers"?

2. What are some ways people get others to follow the rules of their own little kingdom?

3. Explain why so much of the conflict between building our own kingdom and building God's kingdom goes unnoticed.

4. In what way do the "greatest battles take place in the smallest moments"? Do you agree?

5. What are the characteristics of our little kingdoms?

6. How does self-focus lead to self-righteousness?

7. How does self-righteousness lead to self-reliance?

8. How does self-focus lead to self-rule?

9. How does Christ's death on the cross help us to win the battle between living for our little kingdom and truly living for his?

DECIDING MY COURSE ■■■■■■■■■■■■■■■■■■■■■■■■■■■

1. Ask God to reveal to you the values and rules of your own little kingdom for which you live. Write down what he reveals to you. Spend time confessing these to God.

2. In what ways does your own civilization rule in your home?

3. Outside of your home, what are some rules of your little kingdom that you attempt to civilize others in?

4. Identify some ways in which you mix big kingdom standards with your own little kingdom rules.

5. "We say we embrace the transcendent, but where the rubber meets the road in our daily lives, our living shrinks to the field of our personal concerns." Can you relate to this, and does it describe you?

6. Consider the following continuums. Place an X on the continuum where you think others would characterize your life.

Whose "good" drives your daily conversations, desires, and actions?

Your own "good"   The "good" of God's kingdom and others

. . . .

Whose righteousness gives you courage and hope as you deal with daily life?

Focus on your own righteousness   Focus on Jesus' righteousness

. . . .

Whom are you seeking to satisfy?

You live to satisfy yourself.   You live to honor God.

. . . .

Do you live in humble daily community with God and others, admitting your need and seeking help?

You seek to be strong and in control.   You admit your weakness and seek help.

. . . .

Whose rules get the most attention and the quickest response in your life and relationships?

Your own rules   God's standards

. . . .

Whose glory motivates you to do what you do and to say what you say?

Your own glory   God's glory

. . . .

7. Which of the above characteristics do you believe God is currently working most in you to change?

8. When tempted to live for your own kingdom, which of the four gracious provisions cited could you be mindful of to help you in the battle:

- You have the freedom to choose God's kingdom.
- You are forgiven and will never be condemned.
- God's Spirit gives you the power to live for his kingdom.
- You are destined to overcome and win.

Explain how being mindful of these truths will help you to live for God's kingdom?

9. What would your home look and sound like if it were a civilization of God's kingdom?

10. What could you do as a family to "civilize" each other into God's kingdom instead of your own?

POINTS OF INTEREST ■■■■■■■■■■■■■■■■■■■■■■■■■■■

1. Complete **Bible Study Three:** *The Kingdom of Light.*

2. Write your own pledge of allegiance which incorporates the themes of this chapter.

3. Ephesians 5:10 says to "find out what pleases the Lord." Using a concordance, find verses that tell how we can "please" or be "pleasing" to God, that refer to God as being "pleased," and that tell of God's "favor." Organize the verses into themes.

4. Read Romans 6:1–14. What do we gain from being baptized into Christ Jesus? What two things no longer have mastery over us?

5. Take an informal survey. Ask others (spouse, children, coworkers, pastor, neighbors, friends), "What do you think is the most important thing to me?"

6: THE COSTUME KINGDOM

CORE PRINCIPLES ■■■■■■■■■■■■■■■■■■■■■■■■■■■■■

1. As sinners, we can look and act like we are living for God's kingdom while really we are living for our own.
2. God's grace in Christ can rescue us from ourselves.

CHAPTER GOALS ■■■■■■■■■■■■■■■■■■■■■■■■■■■■■■

1. In this chapter, we want to be made aware of how we can look like we are living for God's kingdom but can really be living for ourselves.
2. We want to examine three characteristics that may expose our lives as a masquerade:
    a. a lack of excitement and enthusiasm in the gospel;
    b. disappointment with God; and
    c. taking on the image of our treasures.

■ ■ ■ ■ ■

You Are Here

1. Do you enjoy being in costume? What are some costumes you have worn in your life?
2. What things do you find fulfilling and satisfying?
3. Is there a difference in your excitement toward God between now and when you first came to Christ?
4. What gets you most excited about being a Christian?

Looking at My Destination

1. According to the author, when is the kingdom of self most dangerous?

2. In what way is the kingdom of self a "costume kingdom"?

3. From chapter 4 (and mentioned again in chapter 6), what drives the kingdom of self?

4. What are some forms of "Christianized" idols?

5. Why do we see fruit of the little kingdoms even inside the big kingdom?

6. What are the three things the author cites as fruit of the kingdom of self seen in the church?

7. How does little kingdom living lead to a lack of excitement or enthusiasm in the gospel?

8. What is the principle of Psalm 115?

9. What does it look like to have Christ as your treasure?

10. How do we make the transcendent glories of God a means to an end?

> ■ ■ ■ ■ ■
>
> "AT THE HEART OF IDOLATRY IS THE ATTEMPT TO MANIPULATE 'GOD' OR THE UNSEEN 'SPIRITUAL WORLD' IN ORDER TO OBTAIN SECURITY AND WELL-BEING FOR ONESELF."
> —RAMACHANDRA
>
> ■ ■ ■ ■ ■

DECIDING MY COURSE ■■■■■■■■■■■■■■■■■■■■■■■■■■

1. Do you think it is possible to wear a mask and not really be aware of it? Explain.

2. Identify some earthly treasures that can take on the appearance of spiritual needs?

3. Is your excitement or enthusiasm in the gospel greater than, less than, or the same as when you first began your relationship with God?

4. Do you see your relationship with God as a means to getting what you really want? What are you wanting/expecting in addition to having this relationship?

5. Can you think of a time in the past or present when you felt disappointed with God? What leads to this disappointment?

   How can you apply the ideas from *A Quest for More* to your or another's disappointment?

6. Is there a place in your life where your little kingdom purposes have been masquerading as the kingdom of God?

POINTS OF INTEREST ■■■■■■■■■■■■■■■■■■■■■■■■■■

1. Explain how a kingdom, a civilization, and a masquerade all relate to your life.
2. Draw or explain a satirical cartoon about masks we wear in the kingdom of God.
3. Develop a list of questions you could ask yourself to examine your heart and motives. (For example: Am I excited about this? Why? What will be my response if it does not turn out the way I expect? Does this look like something Christ would do and in this way?) If you discover your heart is wrong, what should you do?

■■■■■

It seems tempting to not do whatever it was you were considering, but that is not always the right thing. Maybe God wants you to do it but wants you to *change your heart*. Confess and repent, then move forward for God's glory and purposes.

Perhaps God has been revealing to you how you have used your relationship with God as a means to getting what you really want. You really have been more focused on your kingdom than his. If you begin to feel discouraged or guilty, you may still have your focus on yourself rather than on God. To keep your focus on God's glory and his kingdom, remind yourself that even your weakness can be to God's glory.

But he said to me, "My grace is sufficient for you, for my power is made perfect in weakness." Therefore I will boast all the more gladly about my weaknesses, so that Christ's power may rest on me. That is why, for Christ's sake, I delight in weaknesses, in insults, in hardships, in persecutions, in difficulties. For when I am weak, then I am strong.

—2 Corinthians 12:9–10

Remember that God loves you, you are forgiven, and you will never be condemned. God's Spirit gives you the power to live for his kingdom. It is a process designed for God's glory!

WHERE HAVE I BEEN ■■■■■■■■■■■■■■■■■■■■■■■■■■■■

Chapters 4–6

1. What two points of focus characterize "little kingdom living"?
2. Both God's kingdom and my personal little kingdom are commitments of the heart. How does this commitment shape the way I respond to everything?
3. In what way are we all kingdom builders, treasure hunters, civilizers, and masqueraders?
4. If someone watched the video of your last year, what treasure would she/he conclude you are after? Material possessions, money, good health, secure future, success, acceptance, power, control, comfort? What can you do so these things are not your treasures?
5. What treasures does Paul say he seeks in Philippians 3:7–14? Can you find other passages of Scripture that define what our treasures should be?
6. Explain why so much of the conflict between building our own kingdom and building God's kingdom goes unnoticed.
7. What are the characteristics of our little kingdoms? Which of those characteristics do you believe God is currently working most in you to change?
8. Explain how being mindful of the following truths will help you to live for God's kingdom: You have the freedom to choose God's kingdom. You are forgiven and will never be condemned. God's Spirit gives you the power to live for his kingdom. You are destined to overcome and win.
9. What are some forms of "Christianized" idols?
10. What are the three things the author cites as fruit of the kingdom of self which are seen in the church?
11. Leader: Answer any questions and read any comments from the cards collected after chapter 5.

SETTING UP CAMP ■■■■■■■■■■■■■■■■■■■■■■■■■■■■■■■

1. Memorize Colossians 1:13–14.
2. Memorize Colossians 2:13–15.
3. How is our small group a means to building God's kingdom?
4. Does our small group look like a civilization of God's kingdom? What could we do to become more "civilized"?
5. For what purpose do you come to small group? Does this purpose need to change?
6. Are we, as a group, enthusiastic about the gospel? Does our time together as a group reflect where our treasure is? Does something need to change?
7. Come up with a list of questions you could ask each other to examine your hearts and motives.
8. Share with the group one thing the Spirit has challenged you with in your past reading.
9. Share with the group one thing the Spirit has encouraged you with in your past reading.
10. How would you answer someone who says it doesn't really matter how we live as long as we are saved and know we are going to heaven?
11. Allow time for people to share what they are learning. Ask if they have done any of the **Points of Interest** and if they would share what has come from that.

7: THE SHRINK DYNAMIC

1. Our lives were meant to connect with God's kingdom.
2. God's kingdom existed before the creation of the world and extends into all eternity, but sin shrinks our desires, motivations, zeal, cares, and concerns down from the size of God's fathomless greatness to the size of our own individual, temporary lives.
3. In our little kingdoms of one, God is squeezed out. However, when we live for God's glories, there is also room for others and room to truly worship God.
4. The kingdom of self is focused on the *here and now*, the *me and mine*, the *wants and needs*, the *physical and material*, and on my *entitlements and rights*.

1. In this chapter, we really want to examine what the author has meant by shrinking our lives to the size of our lives.

2. We want to identify what God intends our lives to be like and identify what characterizes the "shrink-wrapped" life so we can alter our perspective to match God's vision for us.

■ ■ ■ ■ ■

You Are Here

1. When was the last time you meditated on God's greatness?
2. Examine this past week. How are you doing in resisting earth-bound treasures? In overcoming anxiety-bound needs?

Looking at My Destination

1. Explain how sin has "shrink-wrapped" us all.

2. Using the shrink dynamic illustration, describe redemption.

3. What does God intend the size of your life to be?

4. How does living for the fathomless greatness of God affect my relationship with others?

■ ■ ■ ■

WHEN I AM CONTENT

TO LIVE IN MY

LITTLE KINGDOM

OF ONE, IT IS

GOD WHO

GETS SQUEEZED OUT.

■ ■ ■ ■ ■

5. What then are the differences between self-contoured living and God-contoured living?

6. What are the four focuses of a shrink-wrapped life? Contrast each focus with a life that stretches to reach for God's glory.

7. How can I know if what I am enjoying in life is focused on the "here and now"?

8. How can I evaluate if I am spending too much focus on myself?

9. How can I evaluate if my focus is on personal needs and desires?

10. How can I evaluate my balance between the physical and spiritual worlds?

11. How can I evaluate my sense of entitlements and rights?

12. How is reaching out to God and others a means of experiencing true glory and true humanity?

DECIDING MY COURSE ■■■■■■■■■■■■■■■■■■■■■■■■■■■

1. Identify areas during this past week when sin shrank the size of your cares and concerns to the contours of yourself.

2. What are some areas of your life where you would invite God to cut a hole in your shrink wrap and pull you into his kingdom living?

3. Place an X on each continuum where you think it best describes you.

Most of my time, energy, and resources are spent focused on:

Temporary pleasures   Eternal investments
· ·

Most of my time, energy, and resources are focused on:

Myself   Others
· ·

Most of my time, energy, and resources are focused on:

Satisfying my desires   God's desires/needs of others

···

Most of my time, energy and resources are focused on:

Physical appearance   Spiritual growth

···

Most of my time, energy, and resources are focused on:

Protecting my rights and property   Considering others better than myself

···

8: IN THE CENTER OF IT ALL

1. It is not possible to live for God's kingdom and keep yourself at the center.
2. To live for the big kingdom is to live for Christ, and to live for Christ is the only way to be freed from the confines of our little kingdoms and recapture the transcendence for which we were created. In this, we find our true humanity, purpose, and meaning.
3. There is nothing in our lives that does not belong to Christ, and there is no hope apart from the cross of Christ.
4. When Christ is not the center of our lives, we tend to reduce Christianity to theology and rules.
5. When Christ is the center of my life, I am not; and
   a. He becomes the recognized source of everything I am and have.
   b. He becomes the motive to everything I do.
   c. He is what gives my life direction and joy.
   d. He becomes the one thing in which I have confidence.

CHAPTER GOALS ■■■■■■■■■■■■■■■■■■■■■■■■■■■■■■

1. The first goal of this chapter is for us to evaluate who lives at the center of our lives and to recognize that the transcendence we were created for can only exist when Christ is at the center of our lives.
2. The subsequent goal is to place Christ in the center by recognizing him as the source, motive, purpose, and hope in everything we have, do, say, and desire.

■■■■■

You Are Here

1. Describe what it is like being with someone who feels he/she must be the center of everyone's attention and energy.
2. Is it possible to be a Christian and yet exclude Christ? Explain.
3. What are some places or items where the center is prominent or important? What makes the center in each of these examples important? How would you know if Christ was the center of your life?

Looking at My Destination

1. What are some things sin does to us?

2. How do the Old Testament and New Testament connect to tell the story of Christ the King?

3. Is it enough to live for God's kingdom by saying "no" to yourself? Explain. What is the key then to big kingdom living?

4. How does living for Christ lead to transcendence, meaning, and purpose?

5. How does living for yourself actually rob you of your humanity?

> ■ ■ ■ ■ ■
>
> THERE REALLY IS NO PLACE FOR CHRIST IN MANY PEOPLE'S CHRISTIANITY. THEIR FAITH IS NOT ACTUALLY IN *CHRIST*; IT IS IN *CHRISTIANITY* AND THEIR OWN ABILITY TO LIVE IT OUT.
>
> ■ ■ ■ ■ ■

6. What does it functionally mean that the created world was designed to have Christ at the center?

7. Why does the world look at Christ-centered living as foolishness?

8. Why is Christ's crucifixion key to having Christ at the center of our lives?

9. What is the danger of reducing Christianity to theology and rules?

10. What are some replacements for Christ that Christians may live for that look like big kingdom living? Why are these replacements not necessarily true kingdom living?

11. What are the four things Christ needs to be if he is to be the center of your life?

12. What does it mean to see Christ as your source? If Christ is your source, how will you measure your potential?

13. Where can we find God's grace?

14. What does it mean to have Christ as your motive?

15. What does it mean to have Christ as your goal? What does that mean in relation to other goals you may have?

16. What does it mean to have Christ as your hope?

DECIDING MY COURSE ■■■■■■■■■■■■■■■■■■■■■■■■■■■■

1. Does the world's perspective on Christ-centered living influence the way you live? If so, how can you resist and keep Christ at the center?

2. Compare the differences between a Christian who places beliefs and commands at the center to one who has Christ at the center. Which most describes you?

3. Can you identify things in your life where you don't see God as the direct source?

4. Identify areas of your life where there is a greater motivation than Christ.

5. How can having Christ at the center keep you from living for him out of duty?

6. How can having Christ at the center affect the way you make decisions?

7. Which items below are goals you have in your life?

   To be healthy   To have children
   To live comfortably   To be/remain married
   To have smart, healthy, well-behaved children
   To grow in my knowledge of Christ   To show love for Christ in all I do
   To become . . .   To have . . .

8. Which of the goals above do you struggle to submit to God's will?

9. What occupies your mind and controls your dreams?

10. Are you ever manipulative, controlling, or threatening? How can placing Christ as your hope help you resist those behaviors?

■■■■■

As this chapter points out, there is a danger to reducing Christianity to theology and rules; but that can be easy to do—even as you read *A Quest for More* and complete this study. Don't forget that God's greatest purpose for you is to live in Christ through faith. Colossians 2:6 says: "So then, just as you received Christ Jesus as Lord, continue to live in him."

Even Paul described this goal as a "labor" and a struggle, but it is done by God's energy that so powerfully works in us (Colossians 1:29). Christ in you is described as "glorious riches...the hope of glory" (1:27). In Christ are "all the treasures of wisdom and knowledge" (2:3). Therefore, keep your focus on Christ, not on rules and principles.

POINTS OF INTEREST ■■■■■■■■■■■■■■■■■■■■■■■■■■

1. Complete **Bible Study Four:** *A Precious Death*.
2. Relate Colossians 1 to chapter 7 in *A Quest for More*. How does the passage reflect a focus on Christ instead of the "here and now"? On Christ instead of me and mine? On Christ instead of

my own needs and wants? On Christ's entitlements and rights instead of my own?

3. The author describes spiritual truths in very physical terms. Draw a picture that would give a visual representation of the concepts from *A Quest for More* to this point?

9: WELCOME TO YOUR DEATH

CORE PRINCIPLES ■■■■■■■■■■■■■■■■■■■■■■■■■■■■■

1. The pleasures of our little kingdoms promise life, but bring death.
2. The big kingdom requires your death in order to bring life.
3. This death is a death to the pursuit of my priorities, my life, and my plans.
4. This death will bring life because life cannot be found outside of Christ; true life and transcendence cannot be gained when I sit enthroned in my little kingdom.
5. Christ calls us to deny ourselves—to take up our cross and follow him so that we can experience the transcendent life he designed us for—and experience the all-surpassing glory of knowing him.

CHAPTER GOALS ■■■■■■■■■■■■■■■■■■■■■■■■■■■■■

1. In this chapter, we want to understand and then obey Jesus' call to deny ourselves, to take up our cross, and to follow him.

2. We want to accept that this is the only way to experience meaning, purpose, and the transcendent life God has called us to.

■ ■ ■ ■ ■

You Are Here
1. How would you define "living"?
2. Have you ever bought something that didn't work or give you satisfaction like you expected it to?
3. How often do you desire being the best?

Looking at My Destination
1. What is "death pretending to be life"?

2. List some things that pretend to be life but are actually death.

3. What does it look like to deny yourself?

4. What does it mean to take up your cross?

5. The author writes, "Living for the big kingdom of Christ will always require suffering and sacrifice." Why is this so?

6. What does it mean to really follow Christ?

7. Who owns your life?

8. Why does Jesus command us to die to self? Why can't we successfully live in both kingdoms?

9. What does it mean to deny Christ?

10. According to the author, what is the world's best prize?

DECIDING MY COURSE ■■■■■■■■■■■■■■■■■■■■■■■■

1. Is your life invested in pursuing *your* life, *your* wants, and *your* needs?

2. What are you unwilling to sacrifice for the sake of God's kingdom? Your money, your lifestyle, your reputation, your house, your prestige, your car, your esteem from others, your friendships, your plans for the future?

3. Do you live in such a way that your life does not belong to you? In what areas do you continue to fight for self-rule?

4. The author writes, "To jealously hold on to my dream of what I want to accomplish, experience, and enjoy is to guarantee that I will never ever experience true life." Explain this idea.

5. Do you feel spiritually dead? Which parts of the three-fold death have you possibly been unwilling to accept?

6. The author writes, "If I am seeking life outside of the One who is Life, I am effectively committing spiritual suicide. There are more of us out there with these suicidal intentions than not." Do you agree or disagree? What needs to be done so that there are fewer "dying" Christians?

7. Following the author's example of worry, explain how these other areas are often seen as life but really can only lead to death: materialism, success, popularity, and comfort.

> ■ ■ ■ ■ ■
>
> "IF ANYONE WOULD COME AFTER ME, HE MUST DENY HIMSELF AND TAKE UP HIS CROSS AND FOLLOW ME."
>
> —MATTHEW 16:24
>
> ■ ■ ■ ■ ■

8. Do you esteem Christ on Sunday yet invest the passion and action of your life in other treasures during the week?

9. In your everyday situations and relationships, where are you finding it hard to deny yourself, take up your cross, and follow Christ?

POINTS OF INTEREST ■

1. Write an obituary for your "self."
2. A Christian leader from Eastern Europe commented that America has too many *committed* Christians and not enough *submitted* Christians. What is the difference between being a Christian who is committed to Christ and one who is in submission to Christ?
3. Can you write a parable that illustrates the idea of losing something by holding onto it or gaining something by letting it go?

WHERE HAVE I BEEN ■■■■■■■■■■■■■■■■■■■■■■■■■■

Chapters 7–9

1. Explain how sin has "shrink-wrapped" us all.
2. How can I evaluate if my focus is on personal needs and desires in the here and now?
3. How does living for Christ lead to transcendence, meaning, and purpose?
4. How does living for yourself actually rob you of your humanity?
5. What are some replacements for Christ that Christians may live for that look like big kingdom living?
6. Why are these replacements not necessarily true kingdom living?
7. What are the four things Christ needs to be if he is to be the center of my life?
8. Compare the differences between a Christian who places beliefs and commands at the center to one who has Christ at the center.
9. How can having Christ at the center keep you from living for him out of duty?
10. How can having Christ at the center affect the way you make decisions?
11. What does "death pretending to be life" mean?
12. List some things that pretend to be life but are actually death.
13. What does it look like to deny yourself?
14. Why does Jesus command us to die to self? Why can't we successfully live in both kingdoms?
15. According to the author, what is the world's best prize? Have you found this to be true?
16. Explain the following quote: "To jealously hold on to my dream of what I want to accomplish, experience, and enjoy is to guarantee that I will never experience true life."
17. What needs to be done so that there are fewer "dying" Christians?

18. What would it look like to invest your passions and actions each day to Christ?

19. Leader: Encourage your group by reading Hebrews 2:17–18:

> For this reason he had to be made like his brothers in every way, in order that he might become a merciful and faithful high priest in service to God, and that he might make atonement for the sins of the people. Because he himself suffered when he was tempted, he is able to help those who are being tempted.

> What are truths from this passage that can encourage us if we find ourselves falling short?

20. Leader: Read the questions and comments from the cards collected after chapter 8.

SETTING UP CAMP ■■■■■■■■■■■■■■■■■■■■■■■■■■■■■

1. The shrink dynamic can affect a group as well as individuals. Consider the small group or church of which you are a part and answer the continuum items below. Answer first individually and then compare answers as a group. Is there an area(s) where everyone saw a weakness? What can you do to see a change in that area?

   Place an X on each continuum where you think it best describes you.

Most of our time, energy, and resources are focused on:

Temporary pleasures   Eternal investments
....

Most of our time, energy, and resources are focused on:

Ourselves   Others
....

Most of our time, energy, and resources are focused on:

Satisfying our desires   God's desires/needs of others

· ·

Most of our time, energy, and resources are focused on:

Physical appearance   Spiritual growth

· ·

Most of our time, energy, and resources are focused on:

Protecting our rights and property   Considering others
                                                               better than ourselves

· ·

2. Try this as the leader. Bring a plate of cookies or some other desirable food. Place it in the center of the group, covered with shrink-wrap. Discuss the shrink-wrap idea in connection to the plate of food: It is not fulfilling its purpose, which is for others to partake of it. It may seem protected, but it will still get moldy or stale if it stays under wraps. Left to itself, it cannot make others happy, bring joy, or experience what it was designed for.

3. Try to comprehend the scope and extent of your life. Read Matthew 25:34; Ephesians 1:4; Ephesians 2:21–22; Ephesians 3:20–21; Hebrews 11:39–40; and Revelation 22:3–5.

4. A warning label will often explain an item's intended purpose, the possible ways of using it incorrectly, and the possible dangers if it is used incorrectly. If there were a warning label for your life, write what it would say based on chapters 7–9.

5. Allow time for people to share what they are learning. Ask if they have done any of the extension activities and if they would share what has come from that.

10: THE JESUS FOCUS

CORE PRINCIPLES ■■■■■■■■■■■■■■■■■■■■■■■■■■■■■■

1. What we fear and love will rule and shape our lives.
2. Living in the big kingdom requires having Jesus as our focus, which means we fear the Lord, we live according to his Word, and we love him more than anything else.
3. Having Jesus as our focus means
   a. that we are mindful that everything belongs to him;
   b. that who we are and what we have are because of his grace;
   c. that he is great and awesome and ruler over all things; and
   d. that he is just, loving, and merciful.
4. Truly, what we fear and love will rule and shape our lives.

CHAPTER GOALS ■■■■■■■■■■■■■■■■■■■■■■■■■■■■■■

1. This chapter provides us with a more defined meaning of having Jesus as the center of our lives.

2. In this chapter, we want to apply those meanings to our own lives and examine what attitudes, understandings, and actions should shape our lives based on Deuteronomy 10:12–22.

■ ■ ■ ■ ■

You Are Here

List some ideas, terms, or symbols that you think of when you think of a kingdom.

Looking at My Destination

1. In this chapter the author provides a definition of big kingdom living. Write that definition here.

2. Using as few words as possible, according to Deuteronomy 10:12–22, what does God ask of you?

3. What does it mean to fear the Lord?

> ■ ■ ■ ■ ■
>
> THE FEAR AND LOVE
> THAT RULES
> YOUR HEART WILL
> SHAPE YOUR LIFE.
>
> ■ ■ ■ ■ ■

4. Using Deuteronomy 10:12–22, what things should we remember?

DECIDING MY COURSE ■

1. What decision did you make this past week based on fear? Based on fear of the Lord?

2. Is my life characterized by obeying the commands of God's Word? What areas do I need to act on?

3. Be honest, who do you love more—God or yourself? If yourself, why?

4. What percentage of each day is lived in fear of God? In love to God? In obedience to God? Ask God to reveal to you if he wants you to grow in one of these areas.

5. Which of the truths God wants us to remember from Deuteronomy 10 do you have a tendency to forget most often?

What could you do to make that truth a greater part of your life?

11: GROANING

1. Being ungodly is not just about committing a certain list of sins. Being ungodly is also about finding fulfillment outside of God.
2. We should find satisfaction in God alone and not find satisfaction in the things of this world.
3. When we are living for God's kingdom, there should be dissatisfaction in all of us with the way things are in this world.
4. Though God has made all things for his glory and our enjoyment, nothing created was meant to become the satisfaction of our hearts. If it does, we are settling for much less than what God intended for us.
5. Big kingdom living is lived in the tension between deep gratitude and daily groaning.

1. In this chapter we want to challenge where our daily

satisfactions and dissatisfactions lie and use those satisfactions and dissatisfactions as indicators for where our hearts are.

2. We want to rethink our definition of ungodliness and apply that understanding to our lives.

3. We want our satisfactions to lie in Christ alone and not the things of this world.

4. We should be dissatisfied and groan over the state of this world.

■ ■ ■ ■ ■

You Are Here

1. What are some areas or things you feel satisfied with?

2. What are some areas or things you are dissatisfied with?

3. Is there a place for dissatisfaction in the life of a believer?

4. What does it mean to be ungodly?

Looking at My Destination

1. According to the author, what does it mean to be ungodly? (Consider the end of the chapter as well.)

2. What is the problem the author defines with the life of Kat?

3. According to the author, what is the language of those living for big kingdom desires? Why?

4. What is it about our spiritual condition that should cause us to be dissatisfied?

5. What is it about our relationships that should cause us to groan and be dissatisfied?

6. What keeps us from seeking our fulfillment in God alone?

7. How can we be both thankful yet dissatisfied?

DECIDING MY COURSE ■■■■■■■■■■■■■■■■■■■■■■■■■

1. Is your contentment mostly a result of big or little kingdom living?

2. Think about things you are not satisfied with. Do you speak the language of dissatisfaction because of God's kingdom or because of your own kingdom?

3. What aspects, if any, of your well-being are dependent on temporary or physical fulfillment?

How can you shift your dependency from these things to God alone?

4. Rate each of the items below with 1 being low and 10 being high.

How is your desire for spiritual growth?

1   2   3   4   5   6   7   8   9   10

How is your zeal to grow closer to the Lord?

1   2   3   4   5   6   7   8   9   10

How well do you strive to grow in character and faith?

1   2   3   4   5   6   7   8   9   10

How is your sorrow toward the sin and suffering in the world?

1   2   3   4   5   6   7   8   9   10

How is the depth of your personal relationships?

1   2   3   4   5   6   7   8   9   10

Pray and ask God to reveal to you in which of these areas he wants to work in you?

5. Do you view relationships as a means of sharing Christ and his gospel? Which relationship(s) can you more intentionally influence for the sake of sharing Christ?

POINTS OF INTEREST ■■■■■■■■■■■■■■■■■■■■■■■■■■■■

1. Complete **Bible Study Five:** *The Nature of a Kingdom Servant.*
2. Review chapter 10. Read Job 40—41. What is God's purpose in this speech to Job? What and why is God reminding Job of these things?
3. The Psalms present a good example of the tension between satisfaction in God and dissatisfaction with the way of the world. Write your own psalm that expresses both your gratitude to God and your discontentment with the present status quo. (See Psalms 6, 27, 31, 35, 42, 43, 55, 77.)
4. Read Romans 8:22–25. What three actions describe our lives in these verses? What adverbs does Paul use to further describe these actions? What is the difference between groaning "inwardly" and groaning "outwardly"?
5. Read Romans 8:18–39. What are some things Paul mentions about God in these verses that we should find satisfaction in?

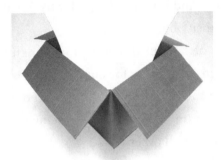

12: JAZZ

CORE PRINCIPLES ■■■■■■■■■■■■■■■■■■■■■■■■■■■■■■■

1. Living for God's kingdom involves both form and freedom.
2. Our lives were designed to submit to the rules and structure God has ordained and revealed to us in his Word.
3. At the same time, however, we are designed to freely express ourselves within that form. We are to use our gifts, our faith, our creativity, and our understandings in variable ways but in harmony with God and others.
4. Living in harmony with God leads to living in harmony with others.

CHAPTER GOALS ■■■■■■■■■■■■■■■■■■■■■■■■■■■■■■■

1. In this chapter, we want to see how big kingdom living is like jazz music—it has both form and freedom.

2. We want to see that not having all the answers can be exciting and beautiful and is God's design for us. We don't want to fear life's spontaneity but to embrace it.

3. We want to be reminded that big kingdom living is not meant to be lived in isolation or for our own desires but is to be lived in community and in harmony with God and with others.

4. We want to examine if our lives are being played in harmony with God and with others.

■ ■ ■ ■ ■

You Are Here

1. If your life were a song, what musical style would it be?

2. Do you prefer spontaneity or regularity? Creativity or simplicity? Form or freedom?

Looking at My Destination

1. How does God want us to play the instrument of our lives?

2. The kingdom, like jazz, is balanced between from and freedom. What do we need to know to follow the form of God's kingdom?

3. Who decides the form and structure of our lives?

4. Why will living within God's structure lead to transcendent living?

5. What is often the problem when there is disharmony in our relationships? What is the solution?

6. In what way are our lives like playing sheet music? In what way is it not like playing sheet music?

7. How are we to use the freedom God has given us to play music with him?

8. Why hasn't God just given us completely scripted sheet music to live by?

DECIDING MY COURSE ■■■■■■■■■■■■■■■■■■■■■■■■■■■■

1. Do you feel like an instrument skillfully played in the hands of God, or are you playing your own tune?

2. Are you in harmony with God? If not, where are you following your own form and structure instead of his?

3. What can you take with you from this chapter so that you can embrace the unsettling spontaneity of life?

■■■■■

Not knowing where we are going or what the exact results of our decisions might be can be unsettling. However, such a life is God's call to us if we desire to allow him to lead by his Spirit. Paul wrote in Romans 8:14–15:

> Those who are led by the Spirit of God are sons of God. For you did not receive a spirit that makes you a slave again to fear, but you received the Spirit of sonship. And by him we cry, "Abba, Father."

Living by the Spirit of God should not be fearful because we know we are his children—loved and precious in his sight. There is no decision we could make that would ever change that.

> For I am convinced that neither death nor life, neither angels nor demons, neither the present nor the future, nor any powers, neither height nor depth, nor anything else in all creation, will be able to separate us from the love of God that is in Christ Jesus our Lord.
>
> —ROMANS 8:38–39

Praise be to God for "the glorious freedom of the children of God!" (Romans 8:21).

WHERE HAVE I BEEN ■■■■■■■■■■■■■■■■■■■■■■■■■■■■■

Chapters 10–12

1. According to Deuteronomy 10:12–22, what does God ask of us?
2. Which of the truths God wants us to remember from Deuteronomy 10 do you have a tendency to forget most often? What could you do to make that truth a greater part of your life?
3. The author writes in chapter 10: "Remembering the Lord is an important discipline of big kingdom, Christ-centered living." How is remembering the Lord a discipline?
4. What is the problem the author defines with the life of Kat? Where should our satisfaction lie? Our dissatisfaction?
5. What does it mean to be ungodly?
6. Which relationship(s) can you more intentionally influence for the sake of sharing Christ? What can the group do to be a part of that work?
7. What aspects, if any, of your well-being are dependent on temporary or physical fulfillment? How can you shift your dependency from these things to God alone?
8. Share with the group which area God is challenging you in: growing closer to the Lord, growing in character and faith, feeling a godly sorrow for sin and suffering, or increasing the depth of your relationships.
9. If your life were a song, what musical style would it be?
10. In what way are our lives like playing sheet music? In what way is it not like playing sheet music?
11. What is often the problem when there is disharmony in our relationships? What is the solution?
12. Why hasn't God just given us completely scripted sheet music to live by?

13. Leader: Read the questions and comments from the cards collected after chapter 11.

SETTING UP CAMP ■■■■■■■■■■■■■■■■■■■■■■■■■■■■■■■■■

1. How is the harmony of your group? What is the form God has designed for your group to follow? Where do you have/should you have freedom? Are members of the group able to use their gifts and abilities?

2. Share with the group one thing the Spirit has been challenging you with from this study.

3. Share with the group one thing the Spirit has been encouraging you with from this study.

13: FORGIVENESS

CORE PRINCIPLES ■■■■■■■■■■■■■■■■■■■■■■■■■■■■

1. Our struggle with forgiveness is a big kingdom struggle. Living for your own kingdom makes it difficult to admit your sin and errors.
2. Asking for forgiveness is letting go of your own way, giving up on your own righteousness, and stepping down from your throne and returning Christ to his rightful place.
3. When you confess, Christ forgives.
4. When you confess, Christ frees you once again from your bondage to yourself so that you can live for him.
5. The big kingdom lifestyle is a lifestyle of forgiveness.

CHAPTER GOALS ■■■■■■■■■■■■■■■■■■■■■■■■■■■■■

1. In this chapter, we want to view our struggle to confess our sins as a battle between our kingdom's success and God's kingdom's

success. Our sin is the result of us wanting our own way, and our unwillingness to seek forgiveness is because we do not want to admit this.

2. We want to know that living in the big kingdom requires a willingness to confess, and we want to be more willing and able to ask for forgiveness in our daily lives.

3. We don't ever want to give up on this battle because Christ fights for us and calls us to it.

■ ■ ■ ■ ■

You Are Here

1. Do you have greater difficulty asking for forgiveness or granting forgiveness?

2. Are you ever tempted to justify your sin?

3. If you invited people to two events, one to protest something and the other to confess something, which gathering do you think would draw the bigger crowd?

Looking at My Destination

1. What leads us to gossip, vengeance, envy, impatience, anger, annoyance, irritation, bitterness?

> ■ ■ ■ ■ ■
> WHEN YOU LIVE
> FOR YOU, YOU
> FORGET GOD AND
> HIS KINGDOM
> AND TRAVEL OUTSIDE
> THE BOUNDARIES
> OF HIS WILL.
> ■ ■ ■ ■ ■

2. According to the author, what makes it so difficult to confess these sins?

3. Why is confession and forgiveness important to living for the big kingdom?

4. What hope do we have in the battle between our kingdom desires and God's?

5. What is the joy that should accompany confession and forgiveness?

DECIDING MY COURSE ■■■■■■■■■■■■■■■■■■■■■■■■■■

1. Do you find joy in seeking forgiveness? Do you understand the joy that should be behind confession and God's forgiveness?

2. Pray and ask God to reveal to you any sins that you should confess.

3. Which of the reminders in the section *Forgiveness and the Big Kingdom* most motivate you to ask for forgiveness?

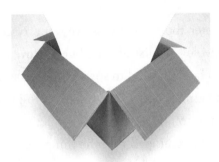

14: LONELINESS

CORE PRINCIPLES ■■■■■■■■■■■■■■■■■■■■■■■■■■■■■■

1. Pursuing a relationship with Jesus as you would a romance is at the heart of big kingdom living. This romance is to give motivation and direction to everything you do.
2. When your heart is not captured by God's astounding love for you and your love for him—no matter how many external Christian pursuits you are giving yourself to—you are still actually living in the little kingdom.
3. Our relationship with Jesus should not just happen in the big moments of life, but rather it takes place in the daily, routine, mundane moments of life.
4. A life driven by affection for Jesus will be a lonely life—not satisfied with anyone or anything taking his place but rather characterized by a longing for his return.

CHAPTER GOALS ■

1. In this chapter about loneliness, we want to see that Christianity is not an ideology or list of rules but is a love relationship.
2. We want to be motivated to spend time with; listen to; and commit our time, energy, and resources to Jesus as we would a loved one and to not run after the seductions of the world.
3. We want to be reminded that the things of this world seek to tempt us away from Christ.
4. We want to accept the fact that, for the Christian, there will be spiritual loneliness since the One we long for is not physically present.

■ ■ ■ ■ ■

You Are Here
1. What is the longest time you have been away from a loved one?
2. What feelings did you experience as you were apart?
3. What feelings did you experience when you were reunited?
4. Are you in control of your schedule, or is your schedule in control of you?
5. Describe what you see and hear when two people are in love.

Looking at My Destination
1. Remind yourself—what drives the life of little kingdom living? (See chapter 4.) According to the author, what drives our lives in the kingdom of God?

2. Describe what makes our lives in the kingdom of God a romance.

3. What is spiritual adultery?

4. Why would a deep love and affection for Christ lead to loneliness?

DECIDING MY COURSE ■■■■■■■■■■■■■■■■■■■■■■■■■■■■■

1. Do you love the Lord more than anything else? Do you think God would like to spend more time with you each day? What prevents you from loving Jesus more than anything else and from spending the time with him that he would want?

How will you fix this problem?

2. If someone watched your daily schedule, what would he/she conclude about what is important to you? Is that what you want to be important?

> ■ ■ ■ ■ ■
>
> "RETURN TO ME, AND I WILL RETURN TO YOU," SAYS THE LORD ALMIGHTY.
>
> —MALACHI 3:7
>
> ■ ■ ■ ■ ■

3. Where in your life are the other "lovers" that compete for your love for Christ? Hobbies? Television? Movies? Sports? Success? Sleep?

POINTS OF INTEREST ■■■■■■■■■■■■■■■■■■■■■■■■■■■■

1. Complete **Bible Study Six:** *The King's Treasure.*
2. Read the following Scriptures: Romans 8:23–25; 1 Corinthians 1:7; Galatians 5:5; and Philippians 3:20. What two words does the NIV use to describe our waiting? What does this kind of waiting look like?
3. Read 1 Thessalonians 1:9–10 and Hebrews 9:28. What will we gain when Christ returns?
4. In John 17:24, Jesus says he wants us to be with him. He too longs to be with us. Why then does he keep us here on earth, and why does he not return? (Consider John 17 and 2 Peter 3:8–9.)
5. Write a letter to Jesus. (Don't just pray, but write because there is something special about writing it down.) Tell him how you are and what you have been up to.

15: SACRIFICE

1. We all have things which we value and are willing to sacrifice for.
2. Christ's sacrifice of his life on the cross sets the model for the sacrifices we are to make in God's kingdom.
3. The control of lesser treasures on our lives leads to destruction—things like anger, anxiety, fear, discouragement, obsession, bitterness, conflict.
4. We are to give up everything to be his disciple so that we can be free from the control and seduction of temporary treasures and live to the fullness of Christ.

1. In this chapter we want to examine the things that may have a hold on our lives.
2. We want to be reminded that Jesus calls us to give up everything in order to be freed from shadow glories.

3. We want to rejoice in the freedom that can come from sacrificing our desires for his.

4. We want to recommit to holding everything in this life with an open hand, willing for God to use and remove those things he wants to.

■ ■ ■ ■ ■

You Are Here

1. What in your life has required a great amount of commitment, discipline, and sacrifice?

2. How many sacrifices do you think you make each day?

3. Do you consider yourself a disciple of Christ?

Looking at My Destination

1. What is the example Christ set for us to live in his big kingdom of life and glory?

2. According to Jesus' teaching in Luke 14, what is required to be his disciple?

> ■ ■ ■ ■ ■
>
> BEHIND EVERY PERSONAL SACRIFICE IS A QUEST FOR SOME KIND OF TREASURE.
>
> ■ ■ ■ ■ ■

3. Why does Jesus require this?

4. Why is a call to sacrifice also a call to freedom?

5. How is both external and internal conflict the result of not giving up everything for Christ?

DECIDING MY COURSE ■■■■■■■■■■■■■■■■■■■■■■■■■■

1. What is it you are holding onto tightly? Your job? Your children? Your reputation? Your health? Money? Time?

2. What was the last conflict you felt or experienced? What lesser treasure were you holding on to?

3. Whose kingdom are you making sacrifices for right now?

WHERE HAVE I BEEN ■■■■■■■■■■■■■■■■■■■■■■■■■■■■■■

Chapters 13–15

1. Tell a time when you felt freed by confessing.
2. According to the author, what makes it so difficult to confess these sins?
3. What is the joy that should accompany confession and forgiveness?
4. Which of the reminders under the section *Forgiveness and the Big Kingdom* most motivate you to ask for forgiveness?
5. What drives the life of little kingdom living? (See chapter 4.) According to the author, what drives our life in the kingdom of God?
6. What is spiritual adultery?
7. Why would a deep love and affection for Christ lead to loneliness?
8. According to Jesus' teaching in Luke 14, what is required to be his disciple? Why does Jesus require this?
9. Why is a call to sacrifice also a call to freedom?
10. In light of all you have read so far, what does it mean when we pray, "Your kingdom come, your will be done on earth as it is in heaven"?
11. Leader: Read the questions and comments from the cards collected after chapter 14.

SETTING UP CAMP■■■■■■■■■■■■■■■■■■■■■■■■■■■■■■■

1. Pray together as a group.
   - Ask the group if there is someone they need to forgive. Ask the group if there is someone they need to ask

forgiveness from. Pray together and encourage each one to
follow through on these issues.
- Ask the group if there are any other issues they need to
  confess, including things that they may love more than Jesus.
- Ask the group if there is anything they feel God is asking
  them to let go of.
- Pray the Lord's Prayer together. (See Matthew 6:9–13.)

2. Evaluate the love you have as a group for Christ. Identify areas that
   you could improve upon. When you meet together, are you just
   following standards and human expectations, or are you meeting
   together with God? What is the difference between the two?
3. How does your time together as a group fulfill Christ's call to
   give up everything and be his disciple?
4. Allow time for people to share what they are learning. Ask if
   they have done any of the **Points of Interest** and if they would
   share what has come from that.

■■■■■

These past three chapters covered forgiveness, loneliness, and sacrifice—
we were reminded of our great neediness. But praise God!

For we do not have a high priest who is unable to sympathize
with our weaknesses, but we have one who has been tempted
in every way, just as we are—yet was without sin. Let us then
approach the throne of grace with confidence, so that we may
receive mercy and find grace to help us in our time of need.

—HEBREWS 4:15–16

16: ANGER

CORE PRINCIPLES ■■■■■■■■■■■■■■■■■■■■■■■■■■■■■■■

1. The Bible is a story of two opposing angers: God is angry because he wants his perfect and holy way accomplished, and man is angry because he wants his way.
2. The two angers cannot co-exist because they are opposed to each other, and God will not forfeit his righteousness.
3. The two angers collide at the cross.
4. The cross rescues us from seeking our own way and to fight for God's cause; to surrender our unrighteous, self-absorbed anger, and to take on God's righteous anger.

CHAPTER GOALS ■■■■■■■■■■■■■■■■■■■■■■■■■■■■■■

1. In chapter 16, we want to surrender our self-absorbed anger and be willing to take up God's anger against sin and injustice.
2. We want to take on the anger of grace that will make us want to do good and to make a difference in the lives of those around us.

3. We want to confess our anger that is caused by selfish desires.

■ ■ ■ ■ ■

You Are Here

1. When was the last time you were angry? Why?
2. Have you ever felt justified in your anger? Why do you feel it was justified?
3. What does anger look and sound like?

Looking at My Destination

1. Explain the difference between biblical propositions and biblical principles.

2. How is the Bible the study of two opposing angers?

3. Where did God's anger finally collide with man's anger?

> ■ ■ ■ ■ ■
>
> CHRIST DIED SO THAT
> YOU WOULD NOT
> BE A CAPTIVE TO
> THE SELF-ABSORBED
> ANGER OF YOUR
> CLAUSTROPHOBIC
> LITTLE KINGDOMS.
>
> ■ ■ ■ ■ ■

4. How can anger be proper in God's kingdom?

5. What defines man's anger? What are the causes? The results?

6. What defines God's anger? What are the causes? The results?

7. Based on the idea of this chapter, what does righteous anger look and sound like? What is the purpose of this anger?

DECIDING MY COURSE ■■■■■■■■■■■■■■■■■■■■■■■■■■■■

1. Have you ever been angry at God? Was your anger misdirected? How could you redirect that anger properly so that it drives you to seek God's righteous cause?

2. What is the response you feel when you consider God's anger poured out on Christ?

3. Have you ever experienced anger that results in mercy, grace, or peace or that leads you to serve or forgive?

4. What kind of anger has a tendency to rule your heart?

5. Do you resign yourself to accepting the sin and suffering around you, or do you allow yourself to get angry and to do something about it?

6. Right now, where you live every day, whose kingdom does your anger serve?

17: HOPE

CORE PRINCIPLES ■■■■■■■■■■■■■■■■■■■■■■■■■■■■■■■■

1. We all put our hope in something.
2. The only hope that will not disappoint is a hope that is in God himself.
    a. A hope that God will fulfill my desires and "needs" is not hope in God but is still hope in my little kingdom.
    b. Hope in God is trusting that whatever he does is best and what he has promised is reliable.
    c. Hope in God is entrusting my past, present, and future and my identity, meaning, and purpose to God's sovereign control.
    d. Hope in God is believing that every promise he has made will be fulfilled and his kingdom will reign forever and ever.
3. Hoping that God will fulfill your will and wishes will probably leave you disappointed; hoping that God will fulfill *his* will and accomplish *his* goal cannot disappoint.

CHAPTER GOALS ■■■■■■■■■■■■■■■■■■■■■■■■■■■■■

1. In this chapter, we want to examine where we have placed our hope.
2. We want to examine why, perhaps, we have felt disappointed.
3. We want to refocus our hopes away from our own kingdom desires and place our hope in Christ and his purposes.
4. We want to be motivated and encouraged by the fact that *God's* kingdom will come, *his will* will be done, and *his* kingdom will be victorious. In this, and in this alone, we can be sure, confident, and full of a hope that will not disappoint!

■■■■■

You Are Here

1. Think back to a time when you were disappointed. What were you hoping would happen that didn't?
2. What leads you to giving up hope?
3. How would you define hope?

Looking at My Destination

1. What are the two classes of hope?

> ■■■■■
>
> YOUR HOPE IS
> ABSOLUTELY ATTACHED
> TO WHAT KINGDOM
> YOU ARE SERVING.
>
> ■■■■■

2. How does the author define/ describe hope?

3. The author writes in reference to Romans 5:1–5: "God's grace even gives us reason to be hopeful right in the middle of suffering." How is it possible to be hopeful even in suffering?

4. According to the author, why doesn't God give us all the things we desire or hope for?

5. The chapter states: "God has not promised to deliver all the things that you have hoped, desired, and convinced yourself that you cannot live without." What are some examples the author gives that God has not promised us and in which we should not place our hope?

   What are some examples the author gives of what God has promised and guaranteed us?

   Can you list some other things God has promised us that we can place our hope in?

6. What is different about hope in God from any other kind of hope?

DECIDING MY COURSE ■■■■■■■■■■■■■■■■■■■■■■■■■

1. In what do you place your hopes?

2. Do you believe that you are already receiving the best things from God's hands? Why or why not?

3. The author writes: "When you wake up with this kind of hope, when it shapes how you deal with people. . . ." How does hope in God affect the way you deal with circumstances, people, and disappointments?

POINTS OF INTEREST ■■■■■■■■■■■■■■■■■■■■■■■■■■■■■

1. Complete **Bible Study Seven:** *Jacob's Rescue.*
2. Read Psalm 62.
3. In verses 1–2, the psalmist writes that his soul finds rest in God and God is his fortress. What are other things that we may look to for rest? For security?
4. Looking at verses 3–4, what troubles does David face?
5. Reread verses 5–8. As king, what other means could David have placed his hope and his honor in?
6. When you face trials and difficulties, do you find hope in your ability to fix it, or do you pour out your heart to God as your hope and refuge? (See verses 9–10.)
7. Why should we not place our hope in others or in riches? What three aspects of God's person does David remind himself of? How can remembering these three qualities help you to place your hope, security, and rest in God alone? (See verses 11–12.)

18: PUTTING IT ALL TOGETHER

CORE PRINCIPLES ■■■■■■■■■■■■■■■■■■■■■■■■■■■■■■■■

1. The kingdom we are living for will shape everything we do, say, decide, and think. Living for God's kingdom gives meaning and purpose to our lives and expands the size of our lives to the size of God's work in the universe.
2. Because God loves us so much and because his cause is holy and righteous, he will not leave us suffocating in our own confined kingdoms.

CHAPTER GOALS ■■■■■■■■■■■■■■■■■■■■■■■■■■■■■■■■

1. In this final chapter, we want to consider the primary truths of *A Quest for More* and take the time to really consider whose kingdom we are living for.
2. We want to celebrate that God wants and is fully able to make our lives transcendent.

■ ■ ■ ■ ■

You Are Here

1. Have you enjoyed reading this book?
2. What questions do you still have that you could pursue the answers for? How will you find the answers to these questions?
3. In what ways has your thinking, your relationship to God, and your lifestyle changed from the truths learned in *A Quest for More* or this Study Guide?

Looking at My Destination

1. How does Zack's life take on the size of God's big kingdom?

2. How does Zack keep the big kingdom in mind even when living "for himself"?

DECIDING MY COURSE ■

1. Take the time to answer the final questions in *A Quest for More*.

2. Which of those questions do you feel God is working on in your life the most?

3. Is God reaching into your life and your heart to pull you outside of your confined world and into the glorious pursuit of living for his kingdom? How is God doing that?

POINTS OF INTEREST ■■■■■■■■■■■■■■■■■■■■■■■■■■■■■■■

1. Hand out cards again. This time, however, have each person write on the card something that will be a reminder to him/her to live for the big kingdom. It could have a key verse, a sentence from *A Quest for More*, or some other creative way for them to remember what their lives are intended to be. Encourage them to place the card somewhere where they will see it often.
2. Pray as a group that each member might be able to share these truths with others. Think of some ways each of you could approach the subject. For example, you could begin by asking someone if he/she believes in God. If so, you can ask what difference God makes in his/her life. This may lead into a discussion about God's vision for our lives.

BIBLE STUDIES

Life in the Garden

What does it mean to be human? Does our definition of being human match God's definition for being human?

■■■■■

When God created Adam and Eve and
placed them in the garden, it may seem their
lives were simple and rather limited. It may seem like
we have so much more today than they ever
would have had. But is this the case?
Read the following passages and
consider what sets man apart from
the rest of God's creation.

■■■■■

■■■■ We are to relate to God and others as a part of God's creation.

GENESIS 1:24; 2:7

- Semantically, there is no difference between men and animals. Both are described as *chay nephesh*—"living creatures."

GENESIS 9:4–10

- God loves and has a purpose for all of his creation. What suggests that all of God's creation is special to him?

COLOSSIANS 1:15–16

- As a part of God's creation, how should we view our relationship to God?

■■■■ There are important differences that make us as humans unique living creatures as revealed to us in the Genesis account. What differences can you identify in the following passages?

GENESIS 1:26–28

- What does it mean to be made in the image of God? Is this unique to men?

- What else sets us apart from the rest of creation?

GENESIS 2:4–5, 15, 19–20

- For what unique purpose do we see God intended for man in these verses?

GENESIS 2:18–24

- Why do you think God created Eve from Adam instead of from the ground like the rest of the living creatures?

- What is uniquely human about the fact that Eve was created to be a suitable helper and that the two were to become united?

- In view of God's relational purpose for Adam and Eve, what might we conclude about God's relational purpose for all people since Adam and Eve were told to be fruitful and to increase in number? (See Genesis 1:28.)

GENESIS 2:16–17; 3:8–11

- What can we see in these passages that is unique about God's relationship to man?

- In light of these purposes for man, do you think we have it better today than life in the garden or worse? What might the world look like today if we consistently followed God's purposes for us?

- How do you think God defines "being human"?

Answer the following question together now as a group before you each read chapters 1–2 in *A Quest for More* for next week: *If you had it "all," what would "all" look like?*

Before you begin this study, do a quick check-up on the group regarding their reading. (See Introduction: What Is a Group Check-Up?)

BIBLE STUDY TWO ■■■■■■■■■■■■■■■■■■■■■■■■■■■■

The Crown of Glory

What is a "crowning achievement"? What has been or do you hope to be your "crowning achievement"?

■■■■■

In Bible Study One, we looked at the purposes God has

for us by looking at what makes us uniquely human. We noticed

that we, as humans, are both a part of creation as well as a

uniquely designed creation. In *A Quest for More*, chapters 1 and 2

describe how we can participate in God's transcendent glories

even now in this fallen world. In this study, we will look at

a future glory that awaits those who are his.

■■■■■

JOHN 17:4–5, 10, 22–24

- According to this prayer, how do we both participate in and share in God's glory? (See also 1 Corinthians 2:7; 2 Corinthians 3:18; 2 Thessalonians 2:13–14.)

- How do we know that Christ had a greater glory waiting for him? (See also Hebrews 2:7–9.)

FIRST PETER 1:6–7; 5:1–4

- How do we know from these passages that there is also a glory for us yet to come? (See also Colossians 3:4.)

ROMANS 8:17–21

- Who groans and waits in "eager expectation"?

- Why does creation groan and for what is it waiting in eager expectation?

SECOND CORINTHIANS 4:16–17
FIRST THESSALONIANS 2:12

- How should our future glory affect how we live now?

If time allows, answer the following questions together now as a group before you each read chapter 3 in *A Quest for More* for next week:

What is often seen as the good life? Is the "good life" different for Christians than it is for non-Christians?

Before you begin this study, do a quick check-up on the group regarding their reading. (See Introduction: What Is a Group Check-Up?)

BIBLE STUDY THREE ■■■■■■■■■■■■■■■■■■■■■■■■■■■

The Kingdom of Light
What does living in God's kingdom look like? What are the "laws" of God's kingdom?

> ■■■■■
>
> In Bible Study Two, we considered the future glory
> that awaits us and how it should affect the way we live now.
> In *A Quest for More*, the author exposes our own little
> kingdoms in chapters 4–6.
> Bible Study Three continues on these ideas
> using the Apostle Paul's letter to the "holy and faithful
> brothers in Christ at Colosse."
>
> ■■■■■

■■■■ As he writes to the church in Colosse, Paul has the kingdom of God in mind. He describes himself as a worker for the kingdom of God (Colossians 4:11) and writes that we "share in the inheritance of the saints in the kingdom of light. For he [God] has rescued us from the dominion of darkness and brought us into the kingdom of the Son he loves" (Colossians 1:12–13). What kingdom/battle imagery does Paul use in Colossians 2:8, 15?

COLOSSIANS 2:13–15

- What word(s) does Paul use to describe the powers and authorities? To describe Christ? To describe us? To describe our sins?

COLOSSIANS 2:16–23

- In light of these truths (vv. 13–15), where should our focus *not* be?

COLOSSIANS 3:1–4

- Where *should* our focus be?

COLOSSIANS 3:5—4:6

- What behaviors and attitudes should *not* characterize life in the kingdom of light?

- What behaviors and attitudes *should* characterize life in the kingdom of light?

- In this kingdom of light, what rules our hearts? What does this look like?

- What does community look like in the kingdom of light? (Consider Colossians 3:11, 16.)

- What does our stewardship look like? (Consider Colossians 3:22—4:2.)

- How does God's truth affect life in this kingdom? (Consider Colossians 2:2–3; 3:2, 9, 10, 16.)

- What other well-known verse talks about "Whatever you do . . ."?

- Can you locate verses in Colossians that remind us that the center and focus of the kingdom is Christ?

- What verses or ideas from Colossians is the Spirit encouraging you with? Challenging you with?

If time allows, answer the following question together now as a group before you each read chapter 6 in *A Quest for More* for next week:

What gets you most excited about being a Christian?

Before you begin this study, do a quick check-up on the group regarding their reading. (See Introduction: What Is a Group Check-Up?)

BIBLE STUDY FOUR ■■■■■■■■■■■■■■■■■■■■■■■■■■■■

A Precious Death

What kind of death can be "precious"? How can we be both free and a servant at the same time?

■■■■■

Bible Study Three considered how life in the kingdom of light

is meant to be lived: focused on Christ and things eternal;

characterized by compassion, kindness, forgiveness, gratitude,

and love; ruled by the peace of Christ; and governed by the

Word of Christ. In *A Quest for More*, chapters 7–9 expand

upon kingdom living and who should be the focus, motivation,

and source of all we do and are as citizens of that kingdom—

Jesus Christ. In this study, we find the same truth as discovered

by someone else and recorded for us in Psalm 116.

■■■■■

PSALM 116

At the initial reading of this psalm, it seems as if the writer faced a deadly situation and is giving thanks to God for rescuing him. However, at a closer reading we find that it is not so much a fatal situation as it is a rescue from a shrink-wrapped life.

- What is the situation from which the writer has been rescued? (Consider vv. 3, 7–8, 16.)

- In this psalm, calling on the name of the Lord seems to be more than just crying out to him for help. Consider verses 2, 4, 13, and 17, and explain what the writer has in mind when he says that he called on the name of the Lord and *will call* on the name of the Lord.

- What are the chains the writer refers to in verse 16? How can he be freed from his chains and yet call himself a servant of the Lord?

- Where might have been the writer's focus before he decided to call on the name of the Lord? (Consider vv. 10–11.)

- If this psalm—as I believe it is—is about a man who shrunk his life to the size of his life, his hope was in men and worldy concerns that left him troubled, in sorrow, and in great need. When he believes (v. 10) and turns back to the Lord, he confesses his affliction and his mistakes (vv. 10–11) and places his trust and hope back on the Lord (*called upon the name of the Lord*). In God's great mercy and compassion, God pulls him out of his kingdom of self (*frees him from his chains*) and restores him to God's glorious kingdom to which he willingly and wisely reclaims his place as servant. In light of this interpretation, what then is the meaning of verse 15?

If time allows, answer the following question together now as a group before you each read chapter 9 in *A Quest for More* for next week:

How would you define "living"?

Before you begin this study, do a quick check-up on the group regarding their reading. (See Introduction: What Is a Group Check-Up?)

BIBLE STUDY FIVE ■■■■■■■■■■■■■■■■■■■■■■■■■■■■■■

The Nature of a Kingdom Servant

Are you in harmony with the Lord and with one another? Where does your focus need refocusing? What characterizes a kingdom servant?

■■■■■

In Bible Study Four, we read about someone who had "shrink-wrapped" his life by limiting his cares and concerns to himself and what the world was offering. In his anguish, he turns back to God who mercifully pulls him out of his shrunken world to live for him. The writer learns that dying to self is true living, true freedom, and precious to God.

In this study, we look at Philippians 2 and relate its truths to the ideas in *A Quest for More*, chapters 10–12. Philippians 2:5–11 may be well-known verses to you, verses that exalt Christ to his rightful place. In this study, we want to relate those well-known verses to the immediate surrounding context and consider Philippians 2:1–18 and how Christ's rightful place should affect our perspective on life.

■■■■■

■■■■ In chapter 10 of *A Quest for More*, the author writes, "Big kingdom living is living with the purpose, character, call, grace, and glory of the Lord Jesus Christ as the central motivation and hope for everything you think, desire, do, and say."

PHILIPPIANS 2:1–18

- What purposes does Paul mention that should place Christ as our focus and motivate our lives?

- What is the character Paul describes that will place Christ as the focus of our lives?

- In chapter 10 of *A Quest for More*, the author says a focus on Christ will be characterized by fear of the Lord, by acting on his commands, and by loving him above all else. Where in Philippians 2:1–18 do you see these principles?

- In this passage, where do you see Paul calling us to be dissatisfied with the status quo? Where do you see that Paul finds his satisfaction/joy in Christ? (Consider vv. 1–2, 17–18.)

- In this passage, where do you see the harmony between God's structure and our freedom? God's part and our part?

■ ■ ■ ■ ■

ROBERTSON TRANSLATES "BEING OF ONE ACCORD" (KJV) AS "HARMONIOUS IN SOUL, SOULS THAT BEAT TOGETHER, IN TUNE WITH CHRIST AND WITH EACH OTHER."

■ ■ ■ ■ ■

- Where do you see that Paul is encouraging us to not write our own musical form or to play our own "notes of autonomy"?

- Paul is calling for unity, not uniformity, in thought. He desires the saints to have a common disposition to work together and serve one another, which is ultimately the humble, servant heart "attitude" of Christ. Are you in harmony with the Lord? With one another? Where does your focus need refocusing?

- We are to have the same attitude as Christ who took on the nature of a servant. As found in this passage in Philippians, what is the nature of a servant in God's kingdom?

If time allows, answer the following question together now as a group before you each read chapter 12 in *A Quest for More* for next week:

If your life were a song, what musical style would it be?

Before you begin this study, do a quick check-up on the group regarding their reading. (See Introduction: What Is a Group Check-Up?)

BIBLE STUDY SIX ■■■■■■■■■■■■■■■■■■■■■■■■■■■■■

The King's Treasure

"What value does the kingdom have to you? Of what value do you think you are to the kingdom?

■■■■■

In this study, we want to see how Jesus viewed the kingdom

of heaven and our place in it. It is two short parables

placed in only three verses. Both are about the kingdom and

both speak about the treasures of the kingdom.

■■■■■

MATTHEW 13:44

- What is Jesus comparing the kingdom to?

- In what way is the treasure—the kingdom of heaven—hidden?

- Who does the man represent? Is his action wise?

- What is Jesus' point in this short parable?

MATTHEW 13:45–46

- What represents the kingdom in this parable? (The comparison to the kingdom in this short parable is not the treasure.)

- Who then does the merchant represent? What does the pearl represent?

- How would you describe the merchant's action?

- How do these two parables fit together?

- If the pearl represents us, how does that make you feel? How does that affect your relationship with the "merchant"?

- Do you respond to and view God's kingdom like the man in verse 44?

- Can you find other Scripture passages that relate to the ideas in these parables?

If time allows, answer the following question together now as a group before you each read chapter 15 in *A Quest for More* for next week:

Do you consider yourself a disciple of Christ?

Before you begin this study, do a quick check-up on the group regarding their reading. (See Introduction: What Is a Group Check-Up?)

BIBLE STUDY SEVEN ■■■■■■■■■■■■■■■■■■■■■■■■■■■■

Jacob's Rescue

How far would God go to rescue us from our meaningless, ephemeral, self-absorbed kingdoms?

■■■■■

Throughout *A Quest for More*, God is celebrated for his gracious

acts of redeeming and rescuing us from ourselves and

the sin that keeps persuading us to live for our own kingdoms.

In this study, we want to observe one of God's such rescues.

It is God's gracious rescue of Jacob from himself.

■■■■■

■■■■ Jacob is an interesting person but not unique. He believes in God but usually feels he needs to maintain some measure of control over his little kingdom. You can find all the events of Jacob's life leading up to Genesis 32 beginning in Genesis 25:19.

GENESIS 32

> *In this portion of Jacob's life, he has run away from his father-in-law Laban's home with his two wives, twelve children, and a large company of servants and livestock. He has successfully manipulated and deceived Laban (Genesis 31:1–3, 20–21),*

but must now face his brother Esau whom he also had deceived and stolen from many years earlier (Genesis 27:41). Jacob is the epitome of little kingdom living. Though he has amassed a large amount of wealth, he has ultimately reduced the size of his life to just the size of his small life.

- Why do you think God sends angels to Jacob?

- What effect does it have on Jacob?

- What is Jacob's emotional state? Why is he so afraid? (See Genesis 27:41.)

- What does Jacob acknowledge and ask in his prayer?

- Does praying change Jacob from needing to be in control?

- Why do you think Jacob then sends his family and the rest of his possessions ahead of him?

- What is Jacob's biggest flaw in all of this?

- Who do you think starts the wrestling match?

- Why does God wrestle with Jacob? Is it necessary?

- Who wins the match?

This, in my opinion, is one of the most fascinating stories recorded for us in the Bible. God comes down and actually wrestles with Jacob! Imagine the scene in heaven.

God speaks: "Jacob, trust me. I said I would be with you and I meant it. Stop trying to take control! Jacob, don't worry about your brother; I'll take care of it. Jacob, there's no need to be so afraid. Jacob, don't send your family. Jacob, I mean it. Jacob, son of Isaac, don't make me come down there!"

But this is the beauty of this event—God does come down. He leaves his throne so he can pull Jacob out of his petty, self-absorbed world. God doesn't need to wrestle with Jacob, and God could have won the battle whenever he wanted; but he didn't. He wanted Jacob's submission and that is finally what he got.

HOSEA 12:3–4
- What further description is given about this wrestling match?

  When God injures Jacob, it is in the form of dislocating his leg. Jacob is no longer wrestling; he is clinging. Jacob was no longer looking to his own strength but to God's. Who wins? Jacob. But Jacob only wins because he submits, and in his submission he gains God's blessing.

- What is your reaction to this wrestling match?

- Have you been aware of ways in which God has tried to get your attention?

- God sent Jacob angels, he spoke to him, and then he finally came down personally to "do business" with Jacob. How is God currently making himself known to you?

- What circumstances has God brought your way to cause you to place your trust and hope in him?

A QUICK WORD ABOUT THE FOLLOWING NOTES ■■■■■■■■■■

The notes are provided to give some idea of answers or possible answers to questions. There are very few answers given to the questions found in **Looking at My Destination** because most of these answers can be found in *A Quest for More*. Answers that require a personal kind of reflection are also not provided. Most of the notes are given in reference to questions that are not present in *A Quest for More* and are not of an individual nature. Notes are provided for every **Bible Study** but not for every chapter. Notes on the Bible Studies are usually very complete and answer most questions.

NOTES ON CHAPTERS 1–3

CHAPTER 1: DECIDING MY COURSE ■ ■ ■ ■ ■ ■ ■ ■ ■ ■ ■ ■

Question 4: What is the difference between someone who lives a purposeful life apart from God and one who lives a purposeful life connected to seeking God's transcendent glories? The difference is that, apart from God, whatever purpose we may live for will be temporary and short of what God intends for us. It is the difference between having a car in your driveway that you take exemplary care of but never leaves the driveway and having a car that you take care of and drive. Your care for your car and the car itself may be admirable, but it falls short of its design and glory if you never drive it. Connecting your purpose to God's glory is like driving a car—it is what you are designed for.

CHAPTER 2: YOU ARE HERE ■ ■ ■ ■ ■ ■ ■ ■ ■ ■ ■ ■ ■ ■ ■ ■ ■ ■

Some legitimate concerns may have to do with providing and caring for your family, relationships that are in conflict, taking care of your property, health, finances, etc.

CHAPTER 2: POINTS OF INTEREST ■ ■ ■ ■ ■ ■ ■ ■ ■ ■ ■ ■ ■ ■ ■ ■

Question 2: How is what Satan offers Jesus "less"? It is less because it is not connected to God's truth or desires. Jesus would be trading his closeness to the Eternal, Almighty Father for the second-rate power of Satan.

Where is Jesus' focus in being able to resist Satan's temptation? (1) the Word of God; (2) on pleasing and trusting the Father

How can we apply this event to our lives in helping us to resist Satan's lies? (1) know the truth from God's Word; (2) know that Satan can be resisted; (3) know that, from Christ's perspective, having God is greater than feeding your forty-day hunger, greater than miracles, and greater than possessing all the kingdoms of the world.

Question 3: How have the people reduced the glory of God to the size of their own lives? They have forgotten all that God has done for them and have limited their focus and concerns upon their own wants. They reject the Lord in favor of going back to Egypt for the sake of food! **What does God do to remind them of the size of his glory?** By bringing the quail, he reminds them that nothing is impossible for God; the plague renews a proper fear of God.

Question 4: How do the actions of the people cause them to lose out on God glory? They lose God's immediate presence; they become a laughingstock to their enemies. **Stewardship glory?** The material wealth God provided them was misused and ultimately destroyed by Moses. **Community glory?** The camp was out of control; the Levites have to mete out punishment upon the people and many are killed. **Truth glory?** They create their own truth (the golden calf); Moses smashes the tablets.

Question 5: What is Jesus teaching us about living for his kingdom?
Living for God's kingdom means serving others.

CHAPTER 3: DECIDING MY COURSE ■■■■■■■■■■■■■■

**Question 1: In what way is an act of disobedience I may commit as
much a catastrophe as Adam and Eve's disobedience?** Any disobedience
I may commit separates me from God and prevents me from participating
in his glory. It may separate me from community with others. It may lead
me to falsehood instead of truth. I may deprive myself of blessing from
God. I forfeit the very purpose of my existence!

CHAPTER 3: POINT OF INTEREST ■■■■■■■■■■■■■■■■■

**How do we see these "ancients" living for God's bigger kingdom and
God's purpose of restoration?** Answers could include: Noah and Abraham
set aside their lives and/or reputations to follow God's commands; Moses'
parents and Moses feared God more than the king. **How do we see that
we are a part of this grand purpose?** "Only together with us would they
be made perfect" (Hebrews 11:40b).

NOTES ON CHAPTERS 4–6

CHAPTER 4: DECIDING MY COURSE ■■■■■■■■■■■■■■

**Question 3: In Matthew 6, Jesus refers to his listeners as "you of little
faith." How does faith play a role in building God's kingdom?** It is often by

faith because God's kingdom cannot be physically seen or touched. Building God's kingdom often requires trusting in God's promises and sovereignty. First John 5:4 says it is our faith that overcomes the world.

CHAPTER 4: POINTS OF INTEREST ■■■■■■■■■■■■■■■■

Question 1: What treasures does Paul say he seeks in Philippians 3:7–14? (1) knowing Christ; (2) the righteousness that comes through faith in Christ; (3) the power of Christ's resurrection; (4) the fellowship of sharing in Christ's sufferings; (5) to attain to the resurrection of the dead.

Question 2: Can you find other passages of Scripture that define what our treasures should be? Some examples include, but are not limited to, the following: God's kindness that leads to repentance (Romans 2:4); the wisdom and knowledge of God (Romans 11:33; Colossians 2:2); the knowledge of the glory of God in the face of Christ (2 Corinthians 4:6).

CHAPTER 5: POINTS OF INTEREST ■■■■■■■■■■■■■■■■

Question 2: Write your own pledge of allegiance which incorporates the themes of this chapter. An example: I pledge allegiance to God's kingdom. I will not seek glory apart from God and will live to follow his kingdom rules and standards, forsaking my own kingdom. I will focus on my own heart and find my righteousness in Christ alone. I will seek to satisfy Christ more than myself.

Question 4: What do we gain from being baptized into Christ Jesus? We are united with him; we may live a new life. **What two things no longer have mastery over us?** death and sin

NOTES ON CHAPTERS 7–9

CHAPTER 8: POINTS OF INTEREST ■■■■■■■■■■■■■■■■

Question 2: Relate Colossians 1 to chapter 7 in *A Quest for More*. How does the passage reflect a focus on Christ instead of the "here and now"? Their faith and love spring from their hope stored up in heaven (v. 5); they give thanks for their inheritance in the kingdom (v. 12). **On Christ instead of me and mine?** their love for the saints (v. 4); bearing fruit in every good work (v. 10) **On Christ instead of my own needs and wants?** Paul's prayer that they would be filled with the knowledge of his will (v. 9); that they might please him in every way (v. 10) **On Christ's entitlements and rights instead of my own?** that Christ would have supremacy in everything (v. 18)

CHAPTER 9: POINTS OF INTEREST ■■■■■■■■■■■■■■■■

Question 1: Write an obituary for your "self." This should not be a dark and gloomy exercise. Have fun with it because this is a death we can rejoice in. Here is an example:

> Today at 7:28 p.m., my "self" died. Nobody will miss him. My
> "self" was controlling, selfish, and proud. At the news of my "self's"
> death, family and friends rejoiced. Jesus has been given control
> of the estate and promises to make all things new. Contributions
> can be made, so that "self" remains dead, by giving words of
> encouragement and accountability.

Question 2: What is the difference between being a Christian who is committed to Christ and one who is in submission to Christ? One can be committed to something or someone but remain in control; that person still decides in what ways he/she will show his/her commitment. One in submission also relinquishes the control.

NOTES ON CHAPTERS 10–12

CHAPTER 11: POINTS OF INTEREST ■■■■■■■■■■■■■■■

Question 2: What is God's purpose in this speech to Job? God is rebuking and correcting Job because Job has questioned God and has not approached God in fear and awe. God is humbling Job. **What and why is God reminding Job of these things?** God is reminding Job that he is only a man and God is God, ruler over everything. God wants to remind Job that he is glorious and majestic, powerful and just. He is reminding Job of his grace, power, and sovereignty in Job's life.

Question 4: What three actions describe our lives in these verses? We groan, wait, and hope. **What adverbs does Paul use to further describe these actions?** We groan inwardly, we wait eagerly, and we hope patiently. **What is the difference between groaning "inwardly" and groaning "outwardly"?** Inward groaning is a spiritual longing and causes us to hope, to wait, to pray, and to depend on God. Outward groaning becomes complaining and would only cause us to seek our own happiness. Outward groaning would be an attempt on our part to fix the problem rather than wait and depend on God.

Question 5: What are some things Paul mentions about God in these verses that we should find satisfaction in? (1) the future glory that will be revealed in us; (2) the future redemption of our bodies; (3) that all things work together for good to those who love him; (4) God is for us;

(5) God will graciously give us all things; (6) Jesus is interceding for us; (7) we are more than conquerors; (8) nothing can separate us from his love

NOTES ON CHAPTERS 13–15

CHAPTER 14: POINTS OF INTEREST ■■■■■■■■■■■■■■■■

Question 1: What two words does the NIV use to describe our waiting? eagerly, patiently **What does this kind of waiting look like?** It almost seems like an oxymoron to be waiting eagerly, but it gives the idea of being expectant and excited. We are waiting for something good to happen. Eager waiting has excitement and joy and hope. One who is waiting eagerly makes sure he/she is ready when the time comes. We are never far from what we are waiting for. Patient waiting does not complain or grumble.

Question 2: What will we gain when Christ returns? We will be rescued from the coming wrath. We will gain salvation.

Question 3: Why then does he keep us here on earth, and why does he not return? God wants everyone to come to repentance. He wants to use us to let the world know that God sent him.

NOTES ON CHAPTERS 16–18

CHAPTER 17: POINTS OF INTEREST ■■■■■■■■■■■■■■■■

Question 2: What are other things that we may look to for rest? Some answers may include family, time alone, a hobby, etc. **For security?** Some answers may include a spouse, family, money, control, etc.

Question 3: Looking at verses 3–4, what troubles does David face? He is being cursed and assaulted and falsely accused.

Question 4: As king, what other means could David had placed his hope and his honor in? David could have placed his hope in an army, his wealth, his position.

Question 6: Why should we not place our hope in others or in riches? They are temporary. They are not as strong and loving as God. They are not our rewards. **What three aspects of God's person does David remind himself of?** God is strong, loving, and just.

NOTES ON BIBLE STUDY ONE

The key idea of this study is to see that we were created for more than just survival and our own self.

PAGE 132, GENESIS 9:4–10, QUESTION 1: What suggests that all of God's creation is special to him? Although God gives animals to man as food, he also holds expectations of the animals. The best way to understand the statement, "I will demand an accounting from every animal," is that even animals will be held accountable if they kill a human. (See also Exodus 21:28.) God also establishes his covenant with man *and* the living creatures that were with Noah.

PAGE 132, COLOSSIANS 1:15–16, QUESTION 1: As a part of God's creation, how should we view our relationship to God? We are his creation. We were created *for him* and he rules over us.

PAGE 132, GENESIS 1:26–28, QUESTION 1: What does it mean to be made in the image of God? Is this unique to men? To be made in God's image does not mean we look like God but rather that we have aspects of his nature: We have emotions, intellect, will, memory, and personality. The greatest difference between man and animal is that man possesses the above attributes in greater measure and that we can possess and use these attributes for reasons *beyond just survival*. **QUESTION 2: What else sets us apart from the rest of creation?** We are to rule over creation.

PAGE 132, GENESIS 2:4–5, 15, 19–20, QUESTION 1: For what unique purpose do we see God intended for man in these verses? Man is to work the ground, take care of it, and name the animals.

PAGE 133, GENESIS 2:18–24, QUESTION 1: Why do you think God created Eve from Adam instead of from the ground like the rest of the living creatures? It is possible that God wanted to create a more special relationship between men and women. **QUESTION 2: What is uniquely human about the fact that Eve was created to be a suitable helper and that the two were to become united?** God was showing that the creation of Adam and Eve and their purpose in the garden was more than just survival. They were to have a social relationship; they were to depend upon each other in a way to help each other. **QUESTION 3: In view of God's relational purpose for Adam and Eve, what might we conclude about God's relational purpose for all people since Adam and Eve were told to be fruitful and to increase in number?** Again, man's life is not just about survival. We are to be in community with others for a greater purpose; we are to care for God's creation and not only ourselves.

PAGE 133, GENESIS 2:16–17; 3:8–11; QUESTION 1: What can we see in these passages that is unique about God's relationship to man? God speaks with them and instructs them; God reveals himself to them and interacts with them; God communicates with man! **QUESTION 2: In light of these purposes for man, do you think we have it better today than life in the garden or worse? What might the world look like today if we consistently followed God's purposes for us?** As seen from God's design for Adam and Eve, we were created to care for creation, to be in community with others, and to receive our guidance and truth from God. There is probably the temptation to think we have it better today because of technology, but we also have lost God's purposes for us. Technology does not reveal truth to us, we cannot socially relate with technology, and we can tend to use technology to only care for ourselves. We have lost harmony with each other, God's creation, and with God himself. **QUESTION 3: How do you think God defines "being human"?** Based on God's design for Adam and Eve, being human is having stewardship over creation, having community with others in a way that is helping others, and having a relationship with God. Anything less is to lose our humanity.

NOTES ON BIBLE STUDY TWO

The key idea of this study is that we share in God's glory, but there is also a glory still in store for us. All of creation eagerly waits for us to receive it and, in light of this future glory, we should live our lives worthy of God.

PAGE 134, JOHN 17:4–5, 10, 22–24, QUESTION 1: According to this prayer, how do we both participate in and share in God's glory? We participate and share in God's glory by being unified and doing the work Christ calls us to do; by receiving and sharing God's wisdom; by being transformed into his likeness so that we reflect his glory; by believing in the truth and being sanctified by the Spirit. **QUESTION 2: How do we know that Christ had a greater glory waiting for him?** We read Christ's words in John 17:5:

"Glorify me . . . with the glory I had with you before the world began." He was made lower than the angels but is now crowned with glory and honor.

PAGE 135, 1 PETER 1:6–7; 5:1–4, QUESTION 1: How do we know from these passages that there is also a glory for us yet to come? 1 Peter 1:6–7: ". . . may result in praise, glory and honor . . ." 1 Peter 5:1–4: "one who also will share in the glory to be revealed"; "you will receive the crown of glory"; Colossians 3:4: "you also will appear with him in glory."

PAGE 135, ROMANS 8:17–21, QUESTION 2: Why does creation groan and for what is it waiting in eager expectation? Creation wants to be liberated from its bondage to decay; creation has been subjected to frustration; creation waits in eager expectation for the sons of God to be revealed.

PAGE 135, 2 CORINTHIANS 4:16–17; 1 THESSALONIANS 2:12, QUESTION 1: How should our future glory affect how we live now? We should not "lose heart" but rejoice in what we will receive; we are to live lives that are worthy of God.

NOTES ON BIBLE STUDY THREE

The key idea of this study is to see that Christ is the center and focus of the kingdom of light and to find some practical ways we are to live in his kingdom.

PAGE 137, COLOSSIANS 2:13–15, QUESTION 1: What word(s) does Paul use to describe the powers and authorities? disarmed, a public spectacle **To describe Christ?** triumphant **To describe us?** alive **To describe our sins?** forgiven

PAGE 137, COLOSSIANS 2:16–23, QUESTION 1: In light of these truths, where should our focus *not* be? false humility, on shadows of things to come, the basic principles and rules of the world, self-imposed worship, human regulations and traditions, human wisdom

PAGE 137, COLOSSIANS 3:1–4, QUESTION 1: Where *should* our focus be? Our focus should be on Christ and on things above, not earthly things.

PAGE 137, COLOSSIANS 3:5—4:6, QUESTION 3: In this kingdom of light, what rules our hearts? the peace of Christ **What does this look like?** Some possible answers are: There will be a lack of worry, a lack of conflict, and love. **QUESTION 4: What does community look like in the kingdom of light?** We are all one; we bear with each other, forgiving each other; we teach and admonish one another. **QUESTION 5: What does our stewardship look like?** We do everything as working for the Lord; it is Christ we are serving. **QUESTION 6: How does God's truth affect life in this kingdom?** We are given the treasures of wisdom and knowledge; we are not to lie to each other; we are being renewed in knowledge; Christ's Word dwells in us.

PAGE 138, QUESTION 7: What other well-known verse talks about "Whatever you do . . ."? 1 Corinthians 10:13 **QUESTION 8: Can you locate verses in Colossians that remind us that the center and focus of the kingdom is Christ?** Colossians 1:15–18; 2:17; 3:4, 11, 17, 24

NOTES ON BIBLE STUDY FOUR

The key idea of this study is to see God's mercy in rescuing us from ourselves and to see that God delights in the "death" of our selves.

PAGE 140, PSALM 116, QUESTION 1: What is the situation from which the writer has been rescued? Although verse 3 talks about the "cords of death" and the "anguish of the grave," it seems as if the situation was not physical death because the writer also describes himself as "overcome by trouble and sorrow." In verse 7, it seems it was his soul that was not "at rest" and he rejoices that his soul was delivered from death, his eyes from tears, and his feet from stumbling. A life or body can be delivered from death, but not our souls, and it seems unlikely to describe physical death as feet that stumble. In verse 16, the writer describes his trouble as being chains from which he was freed. All this seems to point to an affliction other than physical death from which he was rescued. **QUESTION 2: Explain what the writer has in mind when he says that he called on the name of the Lord and *will call* on the name of the Lord.** Although verse 4 seems to have the idea of calling on God for help, this idea does not fit verses 13 and 17 where calling on the name of the Lord is a response of thanksgiving and a way for the psalmist to repay the Lord. The idea of calling on the name of the Lord seems to carry less the idea of needing help and more the idea of placing your hope, your trust, and your life in God's hands. It is more than calling for help; it is calling upon as an act of worship and surrender. **QUESTION 3: What are the chains the writer refers to in verse 16? How can he be freed from his chains and yet call himself a servant of the Lord?** The chains were whatever was troubling him and keeping his soul from being at rest and from living. He is freed from his chains because he is no longer in bondage to the lies of men and whatever was causing his affliction, but he is a servant because he has given himself back to God. **QUESTION 4: Where might have been the writer's focus before he decides to call on the name of**

the Lord? Consider verses 10 and 11. It seems possible his focus was on the world; he bought into the lies of men. His focus was on "living the good life" of the world which he discovers is a lie. **QUESTION 5: What then is the meaning of verse 15?** The writer is not talking about a physical death but a spiritual death to self. This kind of death to self is precious in God's sight.

NOTES ON BIBLE STUDY FIVE

The key idea of this study is that each of us is called to be a servant just as Christ was. We want to see that being a Christian servant means being united with Christ and with others in harmony together, placing others above yourself, serving in God's power without complaining or arguing.

PAGE 143, PHILIPPIANS 2:1–18, QUESTION 1: What purposes does Paul mention that should place Christ as our focus and motivate our lives? Unity, to have the same attitude as Christ, to act according to God's good purposes, so that we might be blameless and pure, that we might shine like stars in the universe. **QUESTION 2: What is the character Paul describes that will place Christ as the focus of our lives?** Humility, being one in spirit and purpose, looking to the interest of others, doing everything without complaining or arguing. **QUESTION 3: A focus on Christ will be characterized by fear of the Lord, by acting on his commands, and by loving him above all else. Where in Philippians 2:1–18 do you see these principles?** Verse 12: "Continue to work out your salvation with fear and trembling" **QUESTION 4: In this passage, where do you see Paul calling us to be dissatisfied with the status quo?** Paul encourages them to work out their salvation, to hold out the word of life, to shine in a crooked and depraved generation. **Where do you see that Paul finds his satisfaction/joy in Christ?** Paul is glad to give up his life for Christ; he looks to the future when he will boast on the day of Christ.

QUESTION 5: In this passage where do you see the harmony between God's structure and our freedom? God's part and our part? God has given Christ as an example of how our attitude should be—considering others better than ourselves. This is a structure for us to live by. We have freedom in being one in spirit and purpose. Our part is to be humble and loving toward others, to not complain and to hold out the word of life; it is God's part to make us shine and to work in us to act according to his will.

PAGE 144, QUESTION 6: Where do you see that Paul is encouraging us to not write our own musical form or to play our own "notes of autonomy"? By encouraging us to be one in purpose, to be like-minded, to have an attitude of humility. **QUESTION 8: As found in this passage in Philippians, what is the nature of a servant in God's kingdom?** It is to consider others better than yourself, to willingly serve others and work alongside others for the same purposes, to not complain or argue, to hold out the word of life, to look to God to work in you to accomplish his will.

NOTES ON BIBLE STUDY SIX

The key purpose of this study is to respond to God's incalculable love for us by surrendering all we have to gain him.

PAGE 145, MATTHEW 13:44, QUESTION 1: What is Jesus comparing the kingdom to? A treasure hidden in a field. **QUESTION 2: In what way is the treasure—the kingdom of heaven—hidden?** It is a spiritual kingdom that cannot be seen; it is hidden because Satan can blind the minds of unbelievers. Even Jesus taught in parables as a means of keeping the truths of the kingdom hidden but also as a way of revealing what was once hidden. **QUESTION 3: Who does the man represent?** Someone who discovers the value of God's kingdom. **Is his action wise?** In the parable, his actions

are wise because he receives more than he gives away—he makes a profit.
QUESTION 4: What is Jesus' point in this short parable? God's kingdom is worth giving up everything you have in order to possess it. (You
may want to point out that Jesus' parables were not necessarily meant to be
dissected in every detail. They are told to convey a main idea and important
truth about the kingdom of God.)

**PAGE 146, MATTHEW 13:45–46, QUESTION 1: What represents the
kingdom in this parable?** A merchant. **QUESTION 2: Who then does the
merchant represent?** Jesus Christ, who gave his life in order to win us. **What
does the pearl represent?** Us, mankind (This may create some questions or
disagreement; study it for yourself and be willing to allow for disagreement.)
QUESTION 3: How would you describe the merchant's action? Some answers may include wise, risky, intentional, etc. **QUESTION 4: How do these
two parables fit together?** We are of great value to God, and God should be
of great value to us.

NOTES ON BIBLE STUDY SEVEN

*The key idea of this study is that God loves us so much that he will do whatever
it takes to get us to submit to him so that we might enjoy the blessings of his
kingdom.*

**PAGE 148, GENESIS 32, QUESTION 1: Why do you think God sends
angels to Jacob?** Possibly to reassure Jacob, remind Jacob that he is with
him, encourage Jacob. **QUESTION 2: What effect does it have on Jacob?**
Seemingly not much; Jacob still seems worried about meeting with Esau.
Note: Jacob's problem is that he does not completely surrender his own
little kingdom; in fact, he calls that place where the angels meet with him
"Mahanaim," which means "two camps," possibly reflecting Jacob's per-

spective that he share control with God. **QUESTION 3: What is Jacob's emotional state?** Fearful. **Why is he so afraid?** Esau had threatened to kill Jacob and held a grudge against him. **QUESTION 4: What does Jacob acknowledge and ask in his prayer?** Jacob acknowledges that it is God who has blessed him. Jacob asks God to save him from Esau. Note: Do you sense a tone of manipulation in this prayer? **QUESTION 5: Does praying change Jacob from needing to be in control?** No, he still attempts to save his family by his own wisdom. **QUESTION 6: Why do you think Jacob then sends his family and the rest of his possessions ahead of him?** Possibly to protect them or possibly to protect himself. **QUESTION 7: What is Jacob's biggest flaw in all of this?** Jacob keeps control instead of relinquishing control to God. **QUESTION 8: Who do you think starts the wrestling match?** We can't really know, but it is interesting to think about. I think it was probably God. **QUESTION 9: Why does God wrestle with Jacob?** God's intention is to get Jacob to submit. **Is it necessary?** It probably is. God knows just what we need and his discipline is perfect. (See Hebrews 12:5–11.) **QUESTION 10: Who wins the match?** God wins because Jacob finally submits to him, but it is also Jacob who wins because his submission wins God's blessing.

PAGE 149, HOSEA 12:3–4, QUESTION 1: What further description is given about this wrestling match? Jacob wept and begged for God's favor.

■ ■ ■ ■ ■

The transcendent glory

that every human being quests for,

whether he knows it or not, is not a thing;

it is a person, and his name is *God*.

■ ■ ■ ■ ■